Coping with Choices to Die

C. G. PRADO

Queen's University, Canada

CAMBRIDGE
UNIVERSITY PRESS

CAMBRIDGE UNIVERSITY PRESS
Cambridge, New York, Melbourne, Madrid, Cape Town, Singapore,
São Paulo, Delhi, Dubai, Tokyo, Mexico City

Cambridge University Press
32 Avenue of the Americas, New York, NY 10013-2473, USA

www.cambridge.org
Information on this title: www.cambridge.org/9780521132480

First published 2011

Printed in the United States of America

A catalog record for this publication is available from the British Library.

Library of Congress Cataloging in Publication data
Prado, C. G.
Coping with choices to die / C.G. Prado.
p. cm.
Includes bibliographical references and index.
ISBN 978-0-521-11476-9 – ISBN 978-0-521-13248-0 (pbk.)
1. Older people – Suicidal behavior. 2. Suicide – Moral and ethical
aspects. 3. Euthanasia – Moral and ethical aspects. I. Title.
HV6545.2.P658 2011
362.28′3–dc22 2010035489

ISBN 978-0-521-11476-9 Hardback
ISBN 978-0-521-13248-0 Paperback

For Catherine, yet again,
and with thanks to:
Wesley Boston for his Foreword and for alerting me to
Norman Doidge's book;
Margaret Battin for a most productive question;
Amber Sharkey for her observations and the
remarks quoted in Chapter 6;
Sandra Taylor for her comments and the remarks quoted in Chapter 6;
Jane Warner for her contribution to the discussion in Chapter 6;
Mel Wiebe for his suggested title;
Rosemary Jolly for putting me on to Soyinka;
and Rouwel Ismail at the Ramada for providing
a much-needed pen at a crucial moment.

There is but one truly serious philosophical problem, and that is suicide.

Judging whether life is or is not worth living amounts to answering the fundamental question of philosophy.

Albert Camus, *The Myth of Sisyphus*
(New York: Vintage Books, 1955), 3

Contents

Foreword

Emotions, Feelings, and Thoughts

Wesley Boston

There are three principal ways to approach an understanding of emotions. One is the philosophical approach, an attempt through conceptual analysis to identify the essence of what emotions are. The second is the psychological approach, which attempts to identify and trace the roles emotions play in peoples' thought and behavior. Philosophers may also draw on the psychological approach for insights to understand the mental mechanisms at play. Different from the philosophical and psychological approaches is the third or neurobiological approach to understanding changes in the brain and body that help to explain emotional experience. The aim of this brief, synoptic account of emotions, and the feelings they cause, is to draw together central insights from these three perspectives to facilitate the treatment of feelings and emotions in the chapters that follow.

THE NEUROBIOLOGICAL APPROACH

Most researchers agree that six primary or basic emotions can be identified: happiness, sadness, fear, anger, surprise, and disgust. Fortunately, today much is known about what happens in the brain and body when one or another of these primary emotions is being experienced. The process is initiated by a stimulus that serves as an adequate inducer. Such a stimulus activates that part of the neural system having to do with emotion.

The system that is activated is composed of both developmentally primitive and more recently evolved areas of the brain.[1] It includes the hypothalamus, the structure at the base of the brain having to do with autonomic control of vegetative functions of the body, such as heart rate; phylogenetically older areas of the cerebral cortex that lie deep within the central part of the brain (the paleocortex); and phylogenetically newer areas at the surface of each brain hemisphere: the prefrontal or orbitofrontal lobes of the neocortex. The system also includes an almond-shaped collection of brain cells lying deep within each hemisphere (within each temporal lobe) called the amygdala, which plays a key role in modulating emotional stimuli. The amygdala receives signals from the hypothalamus and from the paleocortex, and sends signals both back to the hypothalamus and paleocortex and also to the prefrontal areas of the neocortex. In this way the nuclei of the amygdala are involved in the rapid activation of the body's autonomic response to an emotional stimulus, in linking this rapid and unconscious bodily response to the conscious appreciation of its effects on the body, and to the cognitive evaluation of its significance. The integrated collection of both phylogenetically ancient and recent neural tissue that is activated by an emotion-evoking stimulus is known as the limbic system.

One fundamental aspect of the bodily (autonomic and musculo-skeletal) response to an emotion-evoking stimulus is that it is faster than conscious awareness of the bodily changes that occur or the conscious interpretation of these changes. Experimental data suggest that bodily responses to an emotion-evoking stimulus (change in heart rate, muscle tone, secretion of hormones, and mental alertness) are modular and relatively independent of higher cognitive processes.[2] Such a response is also described as an automatic appraisal mechanism that is informationally encapsulated. Moreover, it generally occurs before a belief has been formed and thus the response is referred to as demonstrating the primacy of affect over cognition. As Paul Griffiths observes, bodily responses to an emotion stimulus are

---

[1] Iverson, Susan, Irving Kupfermann, and Eric R. Kandel, 2000. "Emotional States and Feelings." In Eric R. Kandel, James H. Schwartz, and Thomas M. Jessell, eds. *Principles of Neural Science.* New York: McGraw-Hill.

[2] Griffiths, Paul, E. 1997. *What Emotions Really Are: The Problem of Psychological Categories.* Chicago: University of Chicago Press, 91–97.

"mechanisms for saving us from our own intelligence by rapidly and involuntarily initiating essential behaviors" that may be life-saving.[3]

The multiple bodily changes that occur are mapped in the cerebral cortex but not all are raised to consciousness. Antonio Damasio defines the cortical mapping of bodily changes as *feelings*, which, when raised to conscious, he calls "the feeling of a feeling."[4] Damasio contends that it is helpful to restrict the term "emotion" to those physiologic changes in brain and body evoked by an emotion stimulus, and to reserve the term "feeling" to name the private mental experience of an emotion. This understanding makes feeling first-person and only subjectively observable, whereas aspects of an emotion, such as changes in facial expression, are observable by others. I suggest that making this distinction between feeling and emotion is a crucial step toward a clearer philosophical understanding of both feeling and emotion. I turn now to the philosophical approach.

THE PHILOSOPHICAL APPROACH

Philosophical theories of emotion have generally divided into two broad categories: propositional-attitude theories, also called belief-desire or cognitive theories, in which emotions are viewed as psychological events best explained in terms of beliefs and desires; and feeling theories that hold that "emotions are introspective experiences characterized by quality and intensity of sensation" and that "the identity of the emotion depends on this quality."[5] The view that has dominated philosophical thought and writing has been one or another variant of the propositional-attitude or cognitive theory, and the tendency has been to either ignore or discount the role of feelings. For example, Robert Solomon holds that "feelings are never sufficient to differentiate and identify emotions," and Stephen Leighton wrote that "feelings are at best a typical accompaniment to emotions."[6] Charles Taylor did acknowledge the relevance of feelings

---

[3] Griffiths 1997, 95.

[4] Damasio, Antonio, 1999. *The Feeling of What Happens: Body and Emotions in the Making of Consciousness*. New York: Harcourt Brace, 31.

[5] Griffiths 1997, 2.

[6] Solomon, Robert, 1980. "Emotions and Choice." In Amelie Oksenberg Rorty, ed. *Explaining Emotions*. Berkeley: University of California Press, pp. 251–82, 254;

by describing an emotion as something that is experienced or felt about an object or situation, but he insisted that to call the experience an emotion the feeling must be grounded in the judgment about why the object or situation is important.[7]

Peter Goldie is critical of philosophers who either ignore the role of feelings in emotions or regard them merely as "add-ons." He writes that "without feelings emotions would not be what they are" and that belief-desire accounts of emotion "do not do justice to the fundamental importance of feelings in emotional experience."[8] The kind of feeling that Goldie regards as central to emotional experience is feeling that is directed toward the object of the emotion. He calls it "thinking of with feeling" or "feeling towards." He distinguishes feeling towards from bodily feelings, which, for Goldie, are quite simply conscious awareness of changes in one's body. Goldie also argues that thinking of with feeling or feeling towards is distinguishable from believing and not reducible to a combination of believing and desiring, so that an emotion can occur in the absence of a relevant belief. Moreover, he argues that thinking of with feeling or feeling towards is a particular way of grasping the object of an emotional experience that adds content to the thought that is "not fully describable in words."[9]

A question that philosophers ask is whether the folk-psychology concept of emotion constitutes a single object of knowledge or if emotions are merely imposed interpretive categories of little significance. There seems to be a consensus that, as noted, six primary (also called basic or "affect program") emotions can be identified. Each can be described as a coordinated set of changes that constitute a particular emotional response, a response that is complex (incorporates musculoskeletal, organ function, and hormonal changes), automated (changes are involuntarily triggered by the emotion-evoking stimulus), and coordinated: "a stereotypical response involving several body systems."[10] These so-called primary emotional responses are generally believed to have evolutionary origins.

Leighton, Stephen, 2003 "Introduction." In Stephen Leighton, ed. *Philosophy and the Emotions: A Reader*. Peterborough, Canada: Broadview Press, 12.

[7] Taylor, Charles, 1973/1985. "Self-Interpreting Animals." *Human Agency and Language: Philosophical Papers*, I, Cambridge: Cambridge University Press, 45–76.

[8] Goldie, Peter, 2000. *The Emotions: A Philosophical Exploration*. Oxford: Oxford University Press, 50.

[9] Goldie 2000, 61.

[10] Griffiths 1997, 230.

However, the common understanding of emotion also includes phenomena such as shame, jealousy, guilt, and pride, as well as anger that persists for a month or a year without being continuously felt. Moreover, these distinctive and sustained psychological processes may not have immediate and stereotypical behavioral and physiological consequences. Additionally, they appear to be highly integrated with complex, often conscious cognitive processes. These more complex processes are referred to as secondary, social, or higher cognitive emotions and they are interpreted as irruptive patterns of motivation that may deflect a person from a goal derived by means-end reasoning, a matter highly relevant to what follows in the body of this book.[11]

The question that arises at this point is whether higher cognitive emotions are similar to or distinct from primary emotions. The neurobiological view is that a shared biological core underlies all emotional phenomena. An opposing philosophical view is that higher cognitive emotions are so different from primary emotions that they constitute a separate and distinctive psychological category and that the common understanding of emotion as of a single sort should be replaced by one having at least two distinct categories.

EMOTION AND THOUGHT

In addition to whether emotions are best understood in terms of one or more typal categories, another question posed by philosophers is how an emotionally held thought is to be distinguished from a feelingless belief or desire, or how an affective mode of awareness, that is, feeling, is to be distinguished from nonemotional processing of knowledge. Differently put, how is the dichotomy between thought and feeling best explained? As noted, feeling may be defined neurophysiologically as the conscious experience of the mental representation of alterations in bodily state that occur in the having of an emotion and so understood, feeling is inherently self-conscious. In Goldie's account of emotional feeling, which he calls feeling towards, the self-awareness of bodily change is directed at the object or state of affairs that induces the emotion. It is the particular way of grasping the salience of the object of the emotional experience that adds

[11] Griffiths 1997, 243.

content not fully describable in words. It is a primitive grasping of the situation in which primitive refers to both phylogenetic and cognitive mechanisms.

One widely accepted philosophical account of a thought, understood as the objective content and not the process of thinking, is that it is something sharable.[12] On this view, thought is an abstract content that can be an object for one or more minds. In contrast, a feeling towards, as understood by Goldie, is a special kind of awareness. It is thinking of or about something but from an individual's nonsharable point of view. Thinking of with feeling or feeling towards, C. G. Prado suggests, is what individuates a thought, what makes it one's own thought.[13] This take on feeling, and specifically on feeling towards, broadens the concept of feeling put forward by Damasio from that of an inward awareness of changes in bodily state felt as a specific emotion such as fear, to an inwardly directed awareness and an outwardly directed special awareness of the object of emotion. We may say that feeling raised to consciousness is the linking in consciousness of changes occurring in the body with a special awareness of the emotion-evoking object or situation in the environment. It is uniquely personal, directed at once inwardly and outwardly, and nonsharable. It is how some aspect of the world is for the person.

This account fits readily with primary or affect program emotions, but does it also square with higher cognitive emotions in which stereotypical behavioral and physiological consequences seem not to be in evidence? One example of a higher cognitive emotion is shame, such as may come from failure to maintain a moral standard. It will occur in a person with aspirations to dignity, one who can feel her dignity threatened or undermined, and for whom the word "shameful" has meaning. It is an emotion that the person experiences in relation to her existence as a subject and may be called a self-referring emotion. It is also language-dependent and, as Charles Taylor avers, allows for "a fuller and richer articulation of feeling."[14]

---

[12] Frege, Gottlob, 1892. "On Sense and Reference." In Peter Geach and Max Black, translators, eds. *Translations from the Philosophical Writings of Gottlob Frege.* Oxford: Blackwell Press, 62.

[13] Personal communication.

[14] Taylor 1985, 56.

It seems undeniable that feeling is involved in such an experience of shame even though there may be no discernible behavioral or physiological manifestations of what is being felt. It is also undeniable that the feeling is highly integrated with cognitive activity that may lead to long-term planned action. How is feeling to be understood in this case?

It is now known that in some emotional responses the physiological changes that occur are confined to the brain, to alterations in neural mapping that to consciousness feel like bodily changes but may not represent actual changes in body landscape. Damasio calls this the "as if body loop."[15] The person burdened by shame may feel physically dragged down even though there are no recognizable changes in bodily disposition. Based on the most recent findings in neuroimaging studies of emotion, however, it seems reasonable to predict that further refinements in the technology will confirm that there are functional changes in the limbic system of the brain, and possibly in other organ systems as well, when a higher cognitive emotion is being experienced.

Emotions have been described as "the function where mind and body most closely and mysteriously interact," as spanning the divide between mind and body, even as casting doubt on that distinction.[16] I suggest that by understanding the physiological changes that occur in both brain and body as "emotion," and the conscious awareness of these changes as "feeling," and thereby recognizing that emotion and feeling are two sides of the same coin, we better comprehend the intimate relation of mental and physical. When Damasio's physiologic understanding of feeling is merged with Goldie's philosophic understanding of what he calls feeling towards, we better appreciate the combination of conscious awareness of changes in body landscape with heightened awareness of an object or state of affairs in the world and the import of that combination. I suggest that it is this intricate interaction that enables us to be thinking, reaching human beings and that it is what is at the heart of our humanity.

[15] Damasio 1999, 69, 80.
[16] de Sousa, Ronald, 1987. *The Rationality of Emotion*. Cambridge, MA: MIT Press, xvi; Goldie, Peter, and Finn Spicer, 2002. "Introduction." In Peter Goldie, ed. *Understanding Emotions: Mind and Morals*. Aldershot, UK: Ashgate Publishing Limited, 3.

Coping with Choices to Die

1

Laying the Groundwork

This book is about understanding and responding to the choices to die made by persons to whom one is close. Unlike previous books and articles I have written about elective death, or choosing to die rather than continue living in a hopeless and pointlessly punishing manner, this book's main focus is not the reasoning that must be done by individuals for their own choices to die to be rational, though such assessment does figure prominently in what follows.[1] Rather, this book is about the reasoning that needs to be done by the spouses, partners, relatives, and close friends of those who choose to die and how they must adjust their own thinking, perspectives, and attitudes to cope with those choices.

People closely involved with those opting for elective death need to determine on the soundest bases possible if their spouses', partners', relatives', and friends' choices to die should be accepted and if enactment of those choices, whether by negative means such as forgoing

---

[1] Prado, C. G., 1990, *The Last Choice: Preemptive Suicide in Advanced Age*, Westport, CT, and New York: Greenwood Group; 1998, *The Last Choice: Preemptive Suicide in Advanced Age*, 2nd edition, Westport, CT, and London: Greenwood and Praeger Presses; 1999, *Assisted Suicide: Theory and Practice in Elective Death*, with S. J. Taylor, Amherst, NY: Humanity Books; 2000a, *Assisted Suicide: Canadian Perspectives*, ed., Ottawa: University of Ottawa Press; 2000b, "Ambiguity and Synergism in 'Assisted Suicide'," in Prado 2000a, 203–11; 2003, "Foucauldian Ethics and Elective Death," *Journal of Medical Humanities*, special issue, Vol. 24, No. 3–4; 2005, "Suicide and Power," *Symposium*, Vol. 9, No. 1; 2008, *Choosing to Die: Elective Death and Multiculturalism*, Cambridge and New York: Cambridge University Press.

medical treatment or by more proactive methods, should be facilitated or at least not impeded. The other side of the coin is that if their spouses', partners', relatives', or friends' elective-death choices are deemed to be unsoundly reasoned or unacceptably motivated, then there is need to determine whether enactment of the choices should only be discouraged or actively obstructed for the presumed good of those choosing to die.

Determining how one or others should best deal with spouses', partners', relatives', or friends' choices to die has two aspects: one centers on assessment of the elective-death reasoning and motivation of those themselves choosing to die; the other centers on assessment of the reasoning and emotional responses of oneself or others close to the persons choosing to die. To proceed, it is clearly necessary for brevity's sake to shorten references to the people involved on both sides of elective-death decisions, so in what follows I will refer to those individuals themselves choosing to die as "elective-death electors" or more simply as *electors*; I will refer to the spouses, partners, relatives, and friends of electors as "elective-death survivors" or more simply as *survivors*.

Reference to elective-death survivors calls for two qualifications. First, the persons in question will be only potential survivors before electors enacting their choices to die. Also, some may remain potential survivors if electors close to them decide against or postpone enacting their elective-death decisions long enough that they come to be unable to enact them without help, which may take considerable time to obtain because of legal and other obstacles. Nonetheless, potential as well as actual survivors need to deal with electors' decisions, whether those decisions are enacted or not. This is primarily because once they are made, those decisions significantly change the relationships between electors and their spouses, partners, relatives, and close friends.

The second qualification is that it is important that references to elective-death survivors not be taken to include persons involved with electors in a professional role, such as physicians, counselors, and other health-care workers caring for those electors or serving as consultants advising them or assessing their decisions in some expert capacity. The term "survivors," then, will be limited to lay persons having cherished, intimate, or at least very close involvement with electors.

FEELINGS AND EMOTIONS

My last book on elective death, *Choosing to Die: Elective Death and Multiculturalism,* is about the rationality of individuals opting to die in order to curtail the devastating process of drawn-out, tormenting, and often demeaning natural deaths from terminal illness.[2] The focus in that book is on electors' own decisions to die and the reasoning and motivation involved in the making of their decisions. The moment that we consider those close to individuals choosing to die, their survivors, the focus shifts from electors' own reasoning and motivation to how their reasoning, motivation, and decisions are perceived, evaluated, and responded to by their survivors. This shift of focus raises issues that somewhat surprisingly are often more complex than those posed by assessment of electors' own thinking and choices, obviously because the issues involve both electors and survivors rather than only electors. But aside from this obvious fact, the greater complexity is a result of two major factors affecting how elective-death survivors perceive and reason about the choices to die of those close to them and how they deal with anticipated and actual enactment of the choices.

The first of the two factors involves the affective element and is how survivors' feelings and emotions influence their perception of and reasoning about the elective-death decisions of their spouses, partners, relatives, and friends. Survivors cannot deal with even evidently rational choices to die by electors independently of their own feelings and emotions because of the closeness between survivors and electors and the affective element's role in and importance to their relationships with electors. Our feelings and emotions regarding those for whom we care deeply are too integral a part of who we are and how we see things for those feelings and emotions to be successfully set aside in dealing with so momentous an event as a spouse, partner, family member, or close friend willingly choosing to abandon life. There is, then, a pressing need to understand the role of feelings and emotions in how survivors perceive and reason about the choices of electors to embrace death over continuing to live as they are living or expect to continue living. This is why whereas in my

[2] Prado 2008.

previous treatments of elective death the primary concern was with rationality and reasoning, here the primary concern must be with the affective aspect and why there also is need to prioritize – to a point – the affective aspect's role in reasoning.

The feelings and emotions that most notably influence how survivors deal with electors' decisions are of two sorts. The first sort is feelings and emotions centering on electors: particularly survivors' affection for electors and apprehension regarding their best interests and well-being. The second sort of feelings and emotions center on survivors themselves: particularly dread at the loss of someone close and fear that they are not doing enough to help electors or to dissuade them from opting for death. Both sorts of feelings and emotions color every aspect of survivors' consideration of spouses', partners', relatives', or friends' choices to die, and the danger is that they may obstruct understanding of rational and properly motivated decisions or, conversely, may prompt encouragement of ill-reasoned or ill-motivated ones.

Clarity is of the utmost importance in what follows, so it is necessary to make clear how I construe feelings and emotions. Feelings, and especially what Peter Goldie calls "feeling towards," are central to my discussion of survivors' dealing with electors' choices to die and need to be differentiated from emotions in the manner that they are differentiated in Wesley Boston's Foreword.[3] Feelings are what we consciously experience of the bodily goings-on that are the emotions we have and that are diversely stimulated in us and that in turn prompt what we actually feel. This differentiation of feelings and emotions as outlined in the Foreword is crucial to what follows and represents a great deal of work and research, perhaps most notably that of Antonio Damasio.[4]

My references to feelings and emotions, then, are based on the distinction between emotions as bodily goings-on and feelings as conscious awareness of some of those bodily goings-on. However, also

---

[3] Goldie, Peter, 2000, *The Emotions: A Philosophical Exploration*, Oxford: Oxford University Press, 61.

[4] Damasio, Antonio, 1999, *The Feeling of What Happens: Body and Emotions in the Making of Consciousness*, New York: Harcourt Brace; see also Wesley Boston, 2003, *Feeling as the Self-Awareness of Emotion*, Queen's University, Kingston, Ontario. This is Dr. Boston's MA thesis, which I had the privilege of supervising.

central to my treatment of feelings is something that is only tacit in the Foreword's references to Goldie's notion of "feeling towards." This is what Franz Brentano called "intentionality" or the directedness of consciousness on an object.[5] Although this is not the place to pursue the matter in any detail, Brentano focused on intentionality as the defining characteristic of thought or consciousness and attempted to articulate how thought or consciousness is what it is because it is always directed on an object, because it is always thought or consciousness of something.[6] Even when thought or consciousness is self-reflective, it has an object in that it objectifies itself or part of itself.

Brentano's use of the terms "intention" and "intentionality" did not have to do with intention in the sense of meaning or planning to do something. His use of the terms was locative in the sense of how the objects of consciousness are in the mind, but not simply as ideas or images complete in themselves; they are in the mind as representations that reach out to the actual states, things, or events that are what one is conscious of or is thinking about. Brentano's use of "intention," "intentional object," and "intentionality" was an amalgam of the Latin words "in" and "tendere," which when joined together have the sense of "reaching toward." This is just what Goldie tries to capture in using the phrase "feeling towards." Brentano meant to convey how the conscious mind bears on the objects of its thought, whether they are internal states or external things or events.

What is of importance about intentionality or the directedness of consciousness in the present context is that intentional objects may be feelings as well as things or events. The directedness of consciousness may objectify components of consciousness itself, as when we attend carefully to our mood, say, to determine precisely how we feel about something. This is highly significant in the present context because of how much of what follows has to do with focusing and reflecting on feelings both as experienced and as objects of assessment. Crucially, feelings become objects of thought, rather than only being experienced or had, when they are the focus of survivors' consideration

---

[5] Audi, Robert, ed., 1995, *The Cambridge Dictionary of Philosophy*, Cambridge: Cambridge University Press; John Searle, 1987, *Intentionality: An Essay in the Philosophy of Mind*, Cambridge: Cambridge University Press.

[6] I return to intentionality in the Appendix.

of affective influences on their perceptions of and reasoning about electors' choices to die.

Our concern with emotions, as opposed to with feelings, is indirect because emotions are not, as underlying states, intentional objects of consciousness even when they are stimulated in us. Sometimes emotions are experienced in that they cause feeling, but sometimes, perhaps much of the time, they are stimulated but their being so is not evident to those in whom they are stimulated. We often have occasion to say of individuals that they are angry without intending to attribute felt anger to them because while they are angry, at that point they do not realize they are. This can be either because the persons in question are not aware of being angry, though they may be behaving angrily, or because they are experiencing their anger as something else, for instance, merely as frustration or impatience. Most of us have had the experience of snapping at someone, "I'm not angry!" only to realize on doing so that we in fact are angry. Somewhat subtler are cases where for various reasons we dissimulate to ourselves what we actually are feeling. In these cases, friends often enlighten us by observing that, say, our claimed disappointment with something or someone is a considerably higher level of dissatisfaction, or that what we describe as concern for someone's bad luck incorporates a significant amount of satisfaction at their comeuppance.

Again, as affective dispositions, emotions characterize individuals even when they are not stimulated or actualized. Consider that we can and do describe individuals as angry without intending to attribute felt anger or angry feelings to them at the time we describe them as angry. What we usually mean by such an attribution is that the individuals we describe as angry are persons who, though not angry at the moment, are prone to respond angrily to remarks, events, and situations that others treat with equanimity. In this case our attribution has to do with how the individuals in question are more likely to respond angrily to some occurrences than to respond with indifference or patience as others are inclined to do. We apply the description, "angry," to individuals, then, who are not at the moment expressing anger or behaving angrily or, we surmise, feeling anger, in order to convey that they have a disposition to feel anger and to respond angrily to things like imagined slights, transit delays, inconvenient rainstorms, or flat tires, all of which most people find irritating but normally handle without allowing their irritation to rise to the level of anger.

As will emerge, both of the foregoing cases are highly significant to survivors' emotional responses to electors' choices to die. It is often crucial for survivors to be made to understand that they are having certain emotions of which they are not aware or that they refuse to acknowledge or the experience of which they are misconstruing. It is as important that they understand they have certain emotional dispositions the strength of which they may not realize. In the end, we are not so autonomous or self-transparent as conscious entities that we correctly understand all our affective states and cannot be prompted by others to learn about emotional responses we are having but are not aware of, about which we are confused or self-deceived, or about tendencies we have to respond to situations in fixed ways.

In the remainder of this chapter and in those that follow, much of our attention will center on feelings and the role they play in shaping perception and reasoning. Emotions are important here mainly as what prompt feelings and with respect to whether they are accurately reflected in how the feelings prompted are construed. As indicated, throughout what follows I mainly will be discussing feelings, what survivors experience, rather than their emotions as physiological and neurophysiological dispositional states. Reiteration of this point is called for because of our marked tendency to think of feelings and emotions in the ordinary senses in which the terms are used interchangeably and as often as not "emotion" is used simply to designate strong feelings. However, the ordinary senses of "feelings" and "emotions" simply are inadequate to make the points that need to be made about survivors' perceptions and reasoning regarding electors' choices to die.

Much of the need to focus on feelings, on what is experienced of emotions, arises from the fact that survivors' only realistic and effective way of dealing with their emotional reactions to electors' choices is by managing their feelings. Controlling affective influences on survivors' responses to electors' choices to die cannot be a matter of altering their emotions. Altering emotions and factors that stimulate emotions is an impossible task regarding what are described in the Foreword as basic emotions: happiness, sadness, fear, anger, surprise, and disgust. Other emotions are alterable to an extent, but such alteration involves sustained effort and lengthy processes of retraining, whether self-imposed or other-imposed. Survivors' controlling affective influences on their perceptions and reasoning regarding electors' choices to die can only be a matter of their governing the effects of their feelings rather than attempting to change what prompt the feelings.

One thing that considerably complicates consideration of feelings is that as indicated, sometimes survivors' actual emotional reactions to electors' choices are not accurately represented by how they construe their feelings, as when anger masquerades as concern. There is need, therefore, for survivors and those counseling them to identify as clearly as they can just what their real emotional reactions are to spouses', partners', relatives', and friends' elective-death decisions. Only then can survivors understand as well as they need to how their perceptions and reasoning, their judgments and actions, are being influenced by their affective states when electors close to them choose to die.

Another complication is that neither survivors themselves nor those counseling them can rely on what is known about survivors' emotional dispositions to gauge how affective states shape their responses to electors' choices. This is because electors' choices to die usually pose situations in which survivors' emotions and the feelings they prompt do not conform to their long-term affective dispositions. The situations forced on survivors by electors' choices are so different and new that survivors usually are initially at a loss as to how to respond. We will see when we look at culture's role in shaping survivors' responses to electors' decisions that, in like manner, expectations regarding cultural influences on survivors' perceptions of and reasoning about electors' choices also are likely to prove unreliable.

With respect to counseling survivors on the management of their feelings, it is notable that despite common usage failing to differentiate between feelings and emotions as outlined in the Foreword and as I am doing in this chapter, the distinction seems implicit in how we normally deal with feelings. We are prepared to challenge people regarding their feelings at particular times when they are assessing significant situations or making important decisions, but at the same time we are not prepared to challenge them regarding their emotions. This difference amounts to a *de facto* distinction between feelings as short-term, experienced affective states, and emotions as long-term affective dispositions. What is most significant about this common behavior is a key implication in our preparedness to question feelings but not emotions. The implication is that we expect people to have some control of the particular feelings they may have in particular circumstances, but do not expect them to have the same measure of control over their emotions.

We fairly clearly construe emotions or long-term affective dispositions as central to what determines who people are as subjects. David Hume anticipated this recognition of the greater fundamentality of emotions by describing "the passions" or emotions as being "original existence[s] or ... modification[s] of existence" and too fundamental to personality to be altered or curtailed by the application of reason. Hume went further than we want to go, maintaining that all reason can do with respect to the passions is to serve their ends.[7] Hume did not distinguish between emotions and feelings; in his time there was not available to him the concepts and data employed by Damasio and others. I am stressing how emotions, as dispositional states, and feelings, as experienced states, differ in order to best consider how feelings are controllable by the application of reason even if emotions largely are not.

Mention of emotions as determinants of who people are as persons and subjects inevitably raises questions about the second crucial factor operant in how individuals are shaped as persons and how they see elective-death decisions and especially those made by electors close to them. This second factor is culture. The results of acculturation play a hugely important role in individuals' perceptions of and reasoning about elective death to the extent that culture establishes their personal, social, and religious values and beliefs. There is an inescapable interplay between feeling-causing emotions and culture because through behavior modification culture conditions in important ways the long-term affective states that partly make people who

---

[7] Hume, David. 1978. *A Treatise of Human Nature*, Oxford: The Clarendon Press, 414–15.

they are. Reciprocally, emotions play a crucial part in sustaining cultural values and practices.

The primary impact of culture on survivors' perception of and reasoning about electors' decisions mainly has to do with their conceptions of death itself and what are believed to be its consequences when natural or other-inflicted, but especially when self-inflicted. The fundamental questions are whether death is believed to be annihilation of the person as opposed to passage of the person as a soul or spirit to one or another sort of afterlife, and whether its being self-inflicted precludes an afterlife or makes it a daunting prospect.

In *Choosing to Die* and elsewhere I describe rational suicide, and what I am here referring to as elective death, as intentional, uncoerced, and soundly reasoned self-killing. I make clear that to be rational, reasoning about and enactment of suicide must be done in full understanding that death may be and most likely is personal annihilation.[8] One may hope there is an afterlife, but as I have argued, suicide cannot be rational if done with or because of an impossible to substantiate conviction that death is only passage to a different form of existence.[9] Suicide decided and done on that basis amounts to taking a problematic belief as a matter of fact, and doing so precludes or at least seriously qualifies the rationality of choosing to die. It does so because the unsubstantiated conviction about an afterlife compromises the validity of elective-death reasoning by functioning in that reasoning as factual knowledge when it actually is only an unproven belief.[10]

How culture may seriously occlude understanding of elective death as at least likely self-annihilation is most evident when we look beyond our own Western culture to other cultures. For example, the play *Death and the King's Horseman* reflects its author's African culture and provides an apt case in point.[11] In Wole Soyinka's play, characters are portrayed as understanding life and death as cyclical and death as passage from one to another form of continuing existence. The story is about a horseman ready to kill himself, not because he wants

[8] Prado 2008, 49.
[9] Prado 1998, 2008; readers interested in the afterlife issue are encouraged to read the Appendix.
[10] Prado 2008, 76–87; 1998.
[11] Soyinka, Wole, 2002, *Death and the King's Horseman*. New York: W. W. Norton.

to die, but because his king has died and the horseman believes that therefore he also must die in order to continue to serve his king in an afterlife. The horseman's culturally determined worldview impedes, if it does not rule out, his understanding of self-killing as likely or even possibly self-annihilation. Instead the horseman sees ending his own life on the death of his king as necessary to meet his obligations because only by dying himself can he continue to serve his king. The horseman's acculturation, then, most likely would preclude the soundness of his reasoning about elective death by imposing on it an unsubstantiated belief as a factual premise.

Use of the phrase "worldview" in the foregoing paragraph to refer to someone's most fundamental outlook on life poses a problem. While discussing culturally determined perceptions with a colleague, Rosemary Jolly, she used the term "cosmology" to refer to what I just now called a worldview. However, "cosmology" has a narrower sense than "worldview," basically referring to views about the nature of the physical universe. She responded by observing that she felt expressions like "worldview" now have too many different meanings for different people. I agreed with her observation, having heard terms like "philosophy" (used in the colloquial sense), "philosophy of life," "conceptual scheme," and even "Weltanschauung" casually used to refer to attitudes and points of view running the gamut from moral and political ones to those reflecting preferences for "lifestyles" and cuisines, or worse, tendentiously tied to specific belief-sets.

This contemporary ambiguity is unfortunate because I need to refer to how individuals see the world, but in a way not open to overly broad interpretation. I need to refer to the fundamental underlying, dynamic latticeworks of beliefs, values, and principles that determine how individuals construe and order their experience. These are the beliefs, values, and principles that in defining individuals' perspectives and interpretive inclinations, in large measure define those individuals as the persons they are. In what follows, then, I reluctantly will use a neologism I devised to refer to individuals' mostly stable but sometimes changing perspective- and attitude-determining latticeworks or matrices of beliefs, values, principles, and habitual interpretive practices. I will refer to these as individuals' *experience-organizing narratives*, relying on the contemporary use of "narrative" in philosophy and many other disciplines and subdisciplines to designate psychological devices or processes operant in establishing and maintaining self-identity, meaning-determination, and structuring of memory: the interpretational self-told "stories" used to integrate and understand events and occurrences.[12]

For brevity's sake, I will use the acronym "EON" to refer to individuals' experience-organizing narratives: the webs of ideas and dispositions individuals consciously and especially unconsciously use to make sense of what is happening and has happened to them and around them, and on the basis of which they project what will happen to them and around them. As introduced here, the acronym EON refers to particular individuals' experience-organizing narratives, but I also will use it in a collective way to refer to the basic interpretive commonalities that broadly define the EONs of individuals who are members of particular cultures.

Returning to how we do not challenge people's emotions because of their fundamentality to personhood, we need briefly to look at how this understanding has been recently extended and to a point overstated as shared culturally determined elements in our EONs have grown increasingly multicultural, and by "shared culturally determined elements" I here mean EON-influencing cultural elements presently dominant in North America and Western Europe. I should also note that my use of "multicultural" may seem a bit dated to some readers. I am aware that a more recent term is "intersectional," deriving from intersectionality theory. I actually incline to preferring the term "intersectional" because it carries a sense that "multicultural" should carry but often does not: to describe a society as multicultural can mean only that it encompasses a number of different cultures. It is quite consistent with a society being multicultural that there is little or no interaction between component cultures. To describe a society as intersectional, on the other hand, is to strongly imply that its cultural or "sectional" components do, indeed, interact. However, the term may not be familiar to some readers, so to avoid possible confusion, I will use "multicultural" in what follows.[13]

---

[12] Note that there has been a good deal of work and discussion in philosophy and related disciplines about the role of narrative in our lives. See William L. Randall and A. Elizabeth McKim, 2008, *Reading Our Lives*, Oxford and New York: Oxford University Press, especially their bibliography. See also my 1984 *Making Believe: Philosophical Reflections on Fiction*, Westport, CT: Greenwood Press.

[13] See "Intersectionality," 2009, http://en.wikipedia.org/wiki/Intersectionality.

Emphasis on respect for persons regardless of diverse cultural affiliations has contributed significantly to a view I called "cognitive libertarianism" in *Choosing to Die*.[14] This essentially is an intellectually reckless exaggeration of individuals' right to hold diverse opinions and is seen by some as the result of "thoughtless cultural pressure for relativism."[15] The heart of cognitive libertarianism is that "respect for persons requires that everyone has a right to his or her own opinion." This much is perfectly acceptable, but cognitive libertarianism goes further by interpreting the right as entailing that it is morally wrong "to try to force anyone to change his or her opinion." The import of this is that since challenges to and criticism of opinions may prompt changes in them, cognitive libertarianism goes further still and maintains that "it is not morally possible ... to argue against someone's opinion."[16] In the phrasing common among undergraduates, individuals' opinions are "true for them" and hence inviolate.

The logical and conceptual validity of cognitive libertarianism is most dubious.[17] Nonetheless, it is a view held by many and therefore pertinent here to the extent that those same many take it that arguing with electors' about their decisions to die, questioning their reasoning and motivation, is morally prohibited by the requirement that their opinions be respected as an integral part of respecting them as persons.

How cognitive libertarianism affects our considerations is in this way: once it is accepted that people must be respected as persons, it may be further accepted that respect for persons entails unconditional respect for what they think and feel. If so, then what they think and feel specifically about elective death cannot be assessed other than with a view to personal endorsement or rejection. This view confuses respect with uncritical acceptance. Of immediate concern for us is that if this mistaken view prevails, it precludes survivors' rational assessment of electors' decisions to die because it renders electors' reasoning and motivation unchallengeable. It would also follow that we could not assess survivors' own perceptions of and reasoning about electors' choices to die because they, too, would be unchallengeable.

[14] Prado 2008, 91.
[15] Rhem, James, 2006, *The National Teaching and Learning Forum*, 15 (May), 1–4, 4.
[16] Rhem 2006, 4.
[17] Prado 2008, 91–126.

It is crucial to appreciate that while we must respect what people think in respecting them as persons, we cannot simply accept what they think as "true for them" in a sophomoric manner and consider it unchallengeable. It is necessary to see that just as electors' reasoning and motivation must be assessable and assessed, survivors' responses to elective-death choices by their spouses, partners, relatives, and friends must be assessable and assessed if they are to deal rationally and productively with what they face. With respect to emotions and feelings in particular, it is true that in human interactions we take emotions as constitutive elements of who people are and there-fore must respect people's emotions in respecting them. However, although respect for persons and their emotions and the feelings they prompt is a social and moral priority, respect cannot entail uncritical acceptance of the effects emotions and feelings may have on either electors' choices to die or on survivors' perceptions and reasoning regarding electors' decisions.

Cognitive libertarianism aside, we are not prepared always to respect people's emotion-prompted feelings regardless of the con-sequences to themselves and to others. This is especially true when people's lives are at stake. We need to be prepared to question indi-viduals as to how their feelings and emotions may be influencing their reasoning and motivation regarding elective death if they are electors; and if they are survivors, we need to question how their feel-ings and emotions may be influencing their perceptions of and rea-soning about their spouses', partners', relatives', and friends' choices to die.

The core of the limits we impose on how feelings and emotions influence thought and action is that we generally think people should control the impact their emotion-prompted feelings have on their thinking and acting, even if they cannot change what they feel, much less the underlying emotions. We expect reasonableness, and our having this expectation indicates that we believe feelings are under a significant measure of volitional control. We usually see lack of voli-tional control of feelings as self-indulgence, as reprehensible, and sometimes even as pathological. But to say we believe feelings are controllable to a degree is not, of course, to say we believe they can be altered or done away with at will; it is to say only that we believe they can be counteracted. We expect that despite feelings to the contrary, individuals should proceed with courses of action beneficial to themselves or others and refrain from courses of action harmful to themselves or others. Moreover, this expectation increases in strength as the consequences of action increase in significance.

In most cases involving elective death, survivors' emotion-prompted feelings are inescapably important to how they perceive and reason about electors' choices to die. Survivors' feelings significantly affect how they assess electors' reasoning, motivation, and decisions because feelings in large part determine how electors' reasoning, motivation, and decisions look to survivors who have to accept or reject the decisions and live with their consequences. Survivors therefore need to manage their feelings in their own responses to electors' choices to prevent distortions of their perceptions and so of their assessments of electors' reasons and motives.

As I have indicated, much of the following discussion will focus on consideration of the role of survivors' feelings in understanding their spouses', partners', relatives', and friends' choices to die. But as also indicated above, the point is not to try to change survivors' emotional reactions to electors' choices to die; rather, the point is to enable survivors to properly understand those reactions in order to in turn better understand electors' choices and what supports them, and then to respond to those choices in the most reasonable and productive manner. An important part of the objective, then, is to provide discussion and guidelines to enable and assist survivors to identify and control their feelings through probing self-reflection and candid, reasoned discussion with others.

One reason why survivors' reactions to electors' choices to die must be considered carefully is because feelings influencing those reactions sometimes are not readily identifiable by survivors or by those friends or professionals advising them. A particularly notable instance is when feelings present themselves as intuitions or instances of "just knowing": as understandings that, although unsubstantiated, nonetheless are taken as somehow objective. Survivors' emotional responses to electors' decisions too often present the feelings their emotions prompt as externally rather than internally generated, and hence as reliable bases for decisions and actions. It is when feelings present themselves in this way that they may most negatively influence survivors' reasoning, because when they do so feelings are dealt with as perceptions of matters of fact rather than as what they are: the products of emotion.

Misconstrual by survivors of their feelings as intuitions is not something that is usually considered. Part of the reason why it is not is the emphasis on and concern with individual cases where the complexities of dealing with particular problems and situations tend to obscure generalities. This is just one of the problems in trying to deal with elective death without an underlying theoretical framework. But whether noted as such or not, reading feelings as intuitions, translating affective force into cognitive substantiation, can seriously distort survivors' assessments of electors' reasoning and motivation and skew survivors' responses to electors' decisions in an improperly supportive direction. For instance, a survivor's feeling of impending closure, which really manifests suppressed relief at the imminent end of a parent's suffering, may be taken as intuitive realization of the fittingness and timeliness of the parent's abandonment of life and prompt precipitous support of that abandonment. Again, the feeling of impending closure, which manifests the survivor's suppressed relief, may be taken as intuitive realization that the parent will soon be reunited with a deceased spouse and again prompt precipitous support of the parent's choice to die. Of course, misconstrual can work the other way and improperly impede called-for support for electors' choices. Perhaps the most common sort of obstructive misconstrual attributable to spurious intuitions is when survivors' affection and concern for electors cause feelings that present themselves as understanding that electors' choices to die are not necessarily wrong but are hasty. Affection and concern for electors usually carry with them hope for improvement or at least for stability in their conditions, and this hope may manifest itself as a strong feeling, a "knowing," that they are giving up too soon; that their circumstances may get better or not worsen; that they see their situations in too bleak a light because of depression, the effects of medication, or other factors.

Another instance of the consequences of misconstrual of feelings as intuitions, only somewhat less common than the foregoing, is when survivors' affection and concern for electors' prompt denial that they experience as strong feelings or claimed knowledge that electors' choices to die are not a result of genuine hopelessness regarding their conditions and prospects but, rather, a result of misconceived desire not to be burdens or not to cause family and friends further suffering. Still another sort of misconstrual is when survivors' affection-prompted feelings of resentment that electors are choosing to die because selfishly unwilling to bear their conditions a little longer for the sake of more precious time spent with survivors, present themselves as supposed realizations that electors are seeking more attention and do not, in fact, intend to end their lives. Whatever their actual form, survivors' misconstruals of their own feelings essentially preclude proper understanding and appreciation of electors' reasoning and motivation for choosing to die.

The basic problem here is that for affective reasons, survivors may rather easily fail to appreciate electors' actual circumstances and so not adequately understand electors' reasons and motivation for choosing to die. However they actually accomplish it, survivors may convince themselves that they understand electors' circumstances better than electors themselves do, and thereby find cause to precipitously support or misguidedly oppose elective death.

Misconstruals of the foregoing sorts also pose a danger for those who are involved with electors in a professional capacity as physicians or consultants and who must assess the soundness and acceptability of their patients' or clients' elective-death reasoning and motivation. However, in the case of health-care professionals involved with individuals choosing to die, the requirement is that they assess patients' and clients' elective-death reasoning and motivation as objectively as possible, regardless of their own emotions and feelings about elective death in general or in particular cases. Although professionals cannot simply ignore their feelings, they must willfully subordinate those feelings to the sound reasoning and acceptable motivation of electors in their care. It is part of professionals' formal and on-the-job training to learn to maintain an emotional distance from those in their care in order to be objective about patient or client decisions regarding treatment options. The same principle applies to their patients' or clients' decisions about elective death. Admittedly, training is not always sufficient for achieving emotional distance. However, the point is that professionals' personal feelings should influence their dealings with patients and clients choosing to die as little as is humanly possible, and to this extent misconstruals of their feelings are less important, as their feelings must be barred from having an influence regardless of how construed.

The situation is quite different in two crucial ways for elective-death survivors. First, survivors are not bound by professional codes of ethics. Speaking practically, this primarily means they have no explicit institutional governing principles or regulations nor established procedures, much less training, for dealing with elective death. Second, survivors not only cannot be expected to achieve the emotional distance we require of professionals, they cannot be asked to attempt to achieve such distance. As mentioned earlier, this is because doing so would violate the relationships they have with elective-death electors, relationships they value and which partly define them as the persons they are. Although obviously difficult, ways must be found for elective-death survivors to achieve a reasonable measure of objectivity regarding electors' choices to die while not breaching their relationships with electors nor incurring for themselves detrimental psychological consequences resulting from demoralizing objectification of their spouses, partners, relatives, and friends.

Whereas professionals' responses to elective death are guided and conditioned by codes of ethics and training, survivors' responses are prompted and largely determined by love and affection, by mutual trust, and by interdependence. This means that when electors choose to die, unlike professionals who are trained and more objective and so better able to appreciate electors' circumstances, most survivors initially will respond by thinking that electors' choices run counter to their best interests. But when individuals choose to die in terminal illness, that is not the time for those closest to them to oppose their choices in an unthinking, automatic way based on unquestioned assumptions about electors' best interests. That precisely is the time when survivors need to carefully assess the rationality of the electors' decisions in order to properly accept or reject those decisions, and so to respond to them as is most appropriate and productive.

As should now be clear, the problem is that unlike professionals, survivors need to conduct their assessments of electors' decisions while to a significant degree accommodating rather than strictly subordinating their own feelings. Therefore, survivors need to determine as best they can the degree to which their own emotion-prompted feelings color their perceptions of electors' reasoning and motivation. It is crucial for survivors to understand as well as they can manage to do just how their feelings condition their thought and behavior regarding electors' decisions and their enactment. Elective-death survivors owe their spouses, partners, relatives, and friends the fullest understanding they can achieve of their reasons and motives for choosing to die. Survivors also owe themselves the best level of understanding in order to avert negative psychological consequences to themselves.

Professionals caring for the terminally ill, though they may establish close temporary relations with those in their care, do not have a personal stake in the elective deaths of those in their care, though there are two exceptions we need to note. First, a close friend or family member, and even a partner or spouse may be in the capacity of professionally caring for someone choosing to die. However, ethical and legal principles and regulations barring such arrangements ensure that these cases are rare enough not to call for consideration here. Second, professionals may construe their patients' or clients' choices to die as their own personal failures, perhaps because of diagnostic slip-ups on their part, inadequate due diligence in their treatment of those clients and patients, or most likely sheer lack of adequate time for productive consultation. Cases of this sort, though, are an aspect of elective death most relevant to a focus on the roles of professionals and so are not of immediate concern. I mention both of these exceptions only because to not acknowledge them might prompt obstructive questions.

Unlike professionals, survivors decidedly have a personal stake in the elective deaths of those close to them. The consequence is that the elective deaths of spouses, partners, relatives, and friends may well have emotional consequences that affect survivors in seriously negative ways. Even if electors' reasoning and motivation are sound and acceptable to everyone involved with them in whatever capacity, the emotional consequences for survivors nonetheless may be psychologically harmful. Moreover, a somewhat surprising complication is that even when proper understanding of electors' reasoning and motivation is achieved by survivors, its being achieved at the cost of countering strong feelings may later undermine their acceptance of electors' decisions and cause them a good deal of emotional turmoil for having allowed "cold" reason to prevail over powerful feelings.

The regrettable fact is that psychologically injurious emotional consequences for elective-death survivors usually are unavoidable. Survivors need to think of their own interests and may be best advised to recognize and acknowledge that electors' choices to die inevitably produce profound emotional changes in their relationships and to accept those changes. Acceptance may lead to adverse attitudinal shifts, such as anger at a spouse, partner, family member, or close friend for what is felt to be a kind of abandonment. Although these are unfortunate results, they may be preferable to survivors living with corrosive regrets and misgivings because of the termination of relationships they failed or refused to see were essentially ended.

As I have pointed out, what seriously complicates how survivors deal with electors' decisions is that they must accommodate their own feelings and emotions to some extent in responding to those decisions. Survivors cannot try – much less pretend – to achieve rigorous objectivity because their emotions and resultant feelings both define them as persons and are integral to their relationships with electors. Probably the most difficult part of accommodation is that as mentioned earlier, survivors need to appreciate how electors' choices to die change the relationships they have with electors. Survivors must recognize that electors' choices to die radically alter many basic aspects of their relationships with those closest to them. Opting to die rather than endure terminal illness is an inherently self-interested and self-absorbed choice, and it is naive to deny that it is. Choosing to die means serving one's own interests first, even if one does so by forgoing life itself. And choosing to die inexorably means relinquishing relationships with others, and that is something that of course is done before life is actually ended.

The kind of qualitative changes in relationships caused by elective-death decisions are evident to most professionals dealing with terminally ill patients and clients. They are familiar with the most common manifestation of these changes, which is an unacknowledged and usually mutual distancing that occurs between terminally ill individuals and those closest to them. Few people are willing or perhaps able to acknowledge the distancing, but it certainly occurs in one or another form. The distancing is perhaps most evident in a certain artificiality that creeps into how individuals deal with their terminally ill spouses, partners, relatives, and friends. For their part, those who are terminally ill increasingly focus mainly on their own situations and show less and less interest in those of survivors, and given their circumstances, they can hardly be blamed if they do. But the distancing that occurs has a positive side for electors in that it enables them to make their choices regarding elective death more freely. Equally, the distancing may be necessary for survivors' psychological and emotional well-being. Admission of this point is difficult, as it sounds self-serving, but we must keep in mind that survivors face years of continued life and need to manage their responses to electors' choices and deaths in a manner that enables them to cope with the inevitable emotional consequences of electors' choices.

What is of the most immediate importance here about these changes in electors' and survivors' relationships is that the distancing in question may not only be necessary for survivors' psychological well-being, it probably is necessary for them to attain adequate, if not full understanding of their emotional responses to electors' choices and to succeed in controlling their feelings.

Medical science's growing ability to keep people alive means that more and more individuals will find their terminally ill spouses, partners, relatives, and friends deciding they would rather die than continue living as they are living or can expect to continue living. It is increasingly important, then, to help survivors avoid having their feelings negatively bias their perceptions of and reasoning about electors' choices to die so they too readily oppose soundly reasoned and well-motivated elective-death decisions. Conversely, survivors also must be helped to avoid too readily supporting electors' choices that are based on unsound reasoning or unacceptably motivated by problematic religious beliefs or cultural pressures.

There is need for a book like this, then, despite the voluminous literature on suicide and assisted suicide. Many of the books currently available are about the ethical, fiduciary, and social obligations and responsibilities of health-care professionals and of spouses or relatives having discretionary say regarding the treatment of those who decide to end their lives by refusing treatment or more active means. These books tend to focus on the implications for those who are not so much closely involved with those choosing to die as those who are ethically and legally accountable for the circumstances of elective death. Many other books are about the moral and social permissibility of elective death. Still other books do address the psychological and emotional impact on survivors of electors' choices to die, but do so in a mainly reactive manner, being primarily concerned with helping people to cope with elective death after the fact.

In *The Last Choice* and in *Choosing to Die*, I focused on the rationality of elective death.[18] Although this book stands on its own, it basically is a sequel to *Choosing to Die* because while the aim in that book was to demonstrate the rationality of elective death for electors, doing so predictably posed pressing questions about how those close to individuals opting for rational elective death should best respond to their doing so. The aim in this book, then, is to aid elective-death survivors as well as those counseling them and counseling electors in reasoning about electors' grounds for choosing to die so as to rightly accept or reject their choices and to justifiably endorse or impede enactment of those choices.

To close this first chapter, I need to make four clarifications. I then offer a brief summary. The first clarification is that it is imperative to be clear that despite the focus on feelings and emotions, this book is philosophy; it is not a psychological treatise. The book is an abstract investigation of how elective-death survivors must reason about their spouses', partners', relatives', and friends' choices to die in order to accept them as rational and well-motivated or to reject them as inadequately or wrongly reasoned and/or unacceptably motivated.

Second, it must be kept in mind that emotions, as I deal with them in this book, are long-term affective dispositions integral to who individuals are as persons, to what they feel, and to how they act, but are not what individuals actually experience. Emotions are what prompt or cause what is felt. Feelings here are short-term affective experiences; feelings are what individuals know firsthand of their constitutive emotions. Of course, feelings in the present context do not include sensations, such as of heat or cold, pleasure or pain.

Third, when I speak of electors, I mean terminally ill individuals who autonomously choose to end their lives through their own

---

[18] Prado 2008, 1998.

agency; with help, as in assisted suicide; or by requesting euthanasia where that is possible. I am not concerned with individuals choosing to end their lives for other reasons and in other circumstances.

Lastly, this book is addressed to medical ethicists, those in the process of becoming medical ethicists, and especially those who are involved or who anticipate being involved with a spouse, partner, family member, or close friend choosing to die in terminal illness. These latter members of my intended audience are growing in number as more and more people find their lives extended by medicine's increasingly effective techniques but also find the quality of their extended lives unacceptable.

CHAPTER SUMMARY

What complicates elective-death survivors' thinking about choices to die made by electors close to them is how doing so requires more than assessing the soundness of electors' reasoning and the acceptability of their motives. Survivors' understanding of spouses', partners', relatives', and friends' choices to die requires grasping and dealing with how their own feelings condition their perceptions of electors' choices and how their perceptions then condition their reasoning about electors' choices.

There is a pressing need for elective-death survivors both to accommodate their feelings to some degree in responding to electors' decisions and to control their feelings' influences on assessments of the rationality of electors' choices to die. Survivors do not choose to be involved with elective death, but once they are involved, they have no choice but to prudently evaluate electors' choices. Precisely because of their closeness to electors, it is incumbent on them to consider those choices as carefully as they can and to accept or reject them on the soundest bases they are able to achieve. To do otherwise is to diminish their relationships with the spouses, partners, relatives, and friends choosing to die, and to do so at the most inopportune time.

Affective-state complications regarding proper understanding and soundly reasoned assessment of electors' choices to die are considerably worsened by cultural pressures and influences on survivors, which may bias or distort survivors' perceptions of and reasoning about electors' decisions as much as feelings may do. Cultural as well as emotional influences and pressures on survivors' responses to elective death need to be identified and dealt with as rationally as is possible.

My aim in this book is to facilitate survivors' understanding of and sound reasoning about spouses', partners', relatives', and friends' choices to die, and I proceed by looking at how survivors are affected by and might best deal with emotional and cultural influences that inevitably shape their responses to electors' decisions. In the next chapter I look more closely at affective influences on survivors' responses to elective death. I consider the cultural aspect in Chapter 3.

2

Feelings

Their Influences and Control

Elective-death survivors' feelings cannot be approached regarding their management in the same manner as the feelings of health-care professionals. The latter are charged with the well-being of their patients, clients, or consultees, and it is ethically incumbent on them to strive to prevent their feelings from coloring their perceptions and influencing their reasoning. The acknowledged difficulty of meeting this ethical obligation is eased somewhat by the cumulative effect of professionals' routine contact with many patients as well as by the objectivity afforded by their training and expertise. Admittedly, it remains an open question to what extent health-care professionals do effectively counter emotional influences on their perceptions and reasoning when dealing with patients and clients who are facing and making life-and-death treatment decisions, but they seem to do so well enough and, moreover, we have little choice but to take it that they do. But there is good evidence that overall professionals succeed in meeting the ethical challenge, perhaps the best evidence in fact being the frequency with which patients and more often their families complain about physicians and other professionals being too detached when dealing with terminal cases.

In any case, we all have experienced countering our feelings to some degree and thereby in some measure checking the effects of our emotions on what we think and do in circumstances where we need to act in ways that go against our affective inclinations. Moreover, whether or not in a professional capacity, we take it to be part of our being rational that when we need to, we can control our feelings, that we can counter the effects of our emotions to a significant degree, and we tend to think less of people who will not or cannot manage their feelings. The alternative is to succumb to our feelings and thereby surrender our autonomy to emotional pressures, but to do so would be to lessen ourselves as persons.

Although health-care professionals are ethically and occupationally required to put aside their personal feelings in dealing with terminal patients, elective-death survivors cannot be asked or expected to do so. The main reason is that as noted in the previous chapter, survivors' feelings are integral parts of their relationships with electors and overly stringent control of survivors' feeling may well alter or violate those relationships. However, just as important is that for their own sake survivors must accommodate their feelings in some measure when dealing with electors' choices to die, else they risk significant psychological and emotional damage to themselves.

What all of this comes to is that survivors' efforts to be objective regarding affective-state influences on their perceptions and assessments of electors' reasoning, motivation, and decisions must be tempered to a point. Despite survivors owing even those electors closest to them a significant measure of objectivity in assessing their choices to die, survivors cannot simply ignore or indiscriminately contravene their own feelings because those feelings arise from emotional dispositions that are elemental to who survivors are as persons and therefore to who they are as spouses, partners, relatives, and close friends. The problem is, of course, how to accommodate survivors' feelings without overly influencing in negative ways their perceptions of and reasoning about electors' choices to die. Perhaps surprisingly, the solution begins with understanding that we can remake ourselves.

HABIT AND THE CONSTRUCTION OF THE SELF

At this point it is necessary to introduce material that the more practically inclined readers may find too abstract. However, as I argued in *Choosing to Die*, it is necessary to have a sound theoretical basis to enable consistency regarding reasoning about elective death, and developing that basis inevitably involves abstraction. Health-care professionals in particular cannot properly deal with elective death in the way too many now attempt to do, which is on the basis of institutional routines, emulation of senior practitioners, anecdotal models, and debatable personal intuitions.

The importance of a theoretical foundation unfortunately is regularly overlooked or explicitly disparaged.[1] Medical ethicists are well aware of theory/practice tensions due to their straddling the theory/practice divide in their training and work, but even they tend to incline toward the practice side as their experience grows more extensive. The reason that medical ethicists most often give when challenged about this tendency centers on the pressing day-to-day realities they face liaising between terminal patients, their families, and their physicians. These realities are unavoidable, but they do not justify indifference to theory. There is real need for all of those who work directly with the terminally ill to have a solid theoretical basis for dealing systematically with elective-death issues. All I can do here is encourage practically trained and oriented readers to keep an open mind in order to appreciate the importance of material they may initially see as of little relevance to their work because it seems too abstract. My hope is that, on completing this book, even those most resistant to theoretical considerations will recognize their value and importance and, perhaps surprisingly, their applicability.

To continue, my approach to the rationality of elective-death and reasoning about it has been primarily criterial. In *The Last Choice* and *Choosing to Die* I set out criteria for testing elective-death choices and establishing the rationality of some.[2] However, the need to accommodate survivors' feelings in their reasoning about electors' choices to die complicates the criterial approach considerably. It does so because trying to develop criteria for managing affective influences results in a dilemma: if the criteria are general enough to be workable, they reduce to platitudes; but if the criteria are made more specific, they become unworkable because of their number and the number of qualifications each typically requires. A modified approach is needed, then, to enable survivors to systematically establish the soundness of their responses to spouses', partners', relatives', or friends' elective-death decisions.

---

[1] Young, Ernle W. D., 2008, "Choosing to Die: Elective Death and Multiculturalism," *Journal of the American Medical Association*, 300(14), 1703–1704.
[2] Prado 1998, 2008.

Successful modification of the criterial approach has three different though interconnected aspects. The first aspect is conditional in
the sense that it has to do with appreciation and acceptance of the
very idea that feelings can be managed effectively. This first aspect
comes down to individuals needing to recognize that what they feel is
not unalterable because predetermined by their "nature." The second
aspect has to do with achieving the best possible understanding of survivors' feelings and of the influences they exert on their perceptions
of and reasoning about electors' choices to die. As will emerge, this is
a most difficult matter and is not one I can hope to resolve, so for that
reason what follows on this second aspect is more exploratory than
explicatory. The third aspect has to do with how feelings actually may
be managed: how they may be controlled or contravened to insure
that survivors' responses to electors' decisions are as rational as they
can be in the circumstances. It is the first of these three aspects that
requires recourse to the theoretical material that follows.

Management of feelings and their influences begins with grasping
that we are the persons we are because of constructive processes
rather than because of an inherent nature. The import of this is that
we are malleable as persons. It is only when this understanding is
in place that elective-death survivors can productively undertake the
process of managing their feelings and exercising some control over
how those feelings influence their perceptions and reasoning regarding electors' choices to die. It is to enable this understanding that I
have recourse to Michel Foucault's development of the existentialist
insight that existence precedes essence. For Foucault, the self is a product, a construct; it is not an instantiation of a prior existing nature.
Foucault conceives of the self, the subject, as constructed by self- and
other-imposed actions. This conception is at the heart of Foucault's
genealogical works, especially *Discipline and Punish* where he tells us
that "the individual is carefully fabricated ... according to a whole
technique of forces."[3] In *Discipline and Punish* Foucault's reference to
a technique of forces is to the procedures and practices of the prison,
but it soon emerges, especially in his second genealogical work, *The*

---

[3] Foucault, Michel, 1979. *Discipline and Punish*, Alan Sheridan, trans. New York:
Pantheon, 217.

History of Sexuality, that the forces in question are both planned and unplanned and thoroughly permeate our societies, cultures, and practical lives.[4]

Foucauldian genealogy, most briefly put, has nothing to do with tracing familial connections or anything of that sort; it is what some commentators call a domain of analysis. What is often most striking to traditionalists is that genealogy inverts the priority of the significance of the marginal over the ostensibly central; it inverts the priority of the constructed over the supposedly natural; and it inverts the priority of the accidental over the allegedly inevitable in originative accounts. These inversions constitute the core of what is novel in Foucault's thought.[5] What is inverted is the content of historical accounts of allegedly sequential and cumulative events. Foucault's aim is to problematize established histories and understandings of developments by offering alternative accounts of their components. Foucault develops Nietzsche's idea that history is misconceived as "an attempt to capture the exact essence of things," arguing that history is wrongly done if conducted as a search for "origins" in the sense of essential beginnings. Genealogy is the alternative to history so conceived; genealogy "opposes itself to the search for origins."[6] The heart of the idea is that there are no essential sequences to be discerned behind historical developments and that explain why things developed as they did.

The bearing of genealogy on conception of the self is that rather than understanding the self as the natural development of an inherent personality, Foucault understands the self as a construct of varying influences, some planned but most accidental. He rejects the idea that we are the persons we are in virtue of the development or fulfillment of a given nature and sees each of us as products of rearing, culture, and a myriad of influences most of which we cannot begin to trace or identify.

---

[4] Foucault, Michel, 1980, *The History of Sexuality*, Vol. 1, Robert Hurley, trans. New York: Vintage; see also C. G. Prado, 2000c, *Starting with Foucault: An Introduction to Genealogy*, 2nd edition, Boulder, CO, and New York: Westview Press/Perseus Group.

[5] Prado, C. G. 2006, *Searle and Foucault on Truth*, Cambridge and New York: Cambridge University Press, chapter 3.

[6] Foucault 1971, 78, 77.

Conception of the self as constructed, as a product of various influences and practices, is in direct opposition to most earlier and contemporary philosophical conceptions of the self as defined by a given human nature and only made more or less true to that nature by self- and other-imposed practices and influences. It is understanding of the self as a construct that enables productive consideration of how elective-death survivors' feelings may be managed and controlled and their feelings' effects moderated or modified so as to enable survivors to deal as rationally as is humanly possible with electors' choices to die.

The important questions that arise regarding conception of the self as a construct are obvious: what actually is the self if it is constructed; how is the self sustained as a self; and what are the mechanics of the construction of the self? As will emerge these questions have essentially the same answer: we are what we do rather than doing what we do because of being what we are.

To support my presentation of Foucault's conception of the self as constructed instead of nature-determined, I also have recourse to the more familiar thought of a philosopher one does not readily associate with Foucault, namely, John Dewey.[7] But as is so often the case in philosophy, discussing how Foucault and Dewey understand the construction of the self inevitably takes us to Aristotle. This is because underlying and enabling Foucault and Dewey's views of the self and how it is constructed is the key idea of habit formation and its effects on persons.

While it certainly antedates Aristotle and is implicit in aspects of Plato's work, the idea of habit formation's role in the construction of the self is first most clearly and succinctly articulated by Aristotle, who tells us that "A state [of character] arises from [the repetition of] similar activities."[8] For Aristotle, as for Foucault and Dewey, you become and are what you consistently do.

What Foucault and Dewey add to the Aristotelian idea of how habit formation constructs selves and thereby shapes persons is the role of

[7] Prado, C. G., "Educating the Self: Dewey and Foucault," forthcoming in Paul Fairfield, ed., *Dewey and Continental Philosophy*, Carbondale: University of Southern Illinois Press.

[8] Aristotle, 1985, *Nicomachean Ethics*, Terence Irwin, trans., Indianapolis: Hackett Publications, 1103b, 35.

others in individuals' acquisition of habits. Foucault approaches the role of others in terms of both the deliberate and the inadvertent results of the disciplining of individuals by institutions that impose regimens, schedules, and duties on them, as well as the intended and unintended impact of other people's conduct on that disciplining.[9] Although Foucault attributes discipline to all institutions, he concerns himself particularly with its use in the prison, the factory, and the clinic or hospital, focusing on three fundamental methods of control of behavior and imposition of subservience: observation, normalization, and examination.[10] What this amounts to is that individuals are disciplined in Foucault's sense by being constantly watched – or being made to believe they are constantly watched; by being intimidated or otherwise compelled to adhere to established standards of behavior – some of which is compulsory; and by being constantly questioned to measure compliance and to elicit instances and sources of resistance.

For his part, Dewey focuses on the school and approaches the role of others in habit formation in terms of planned and implemented educational routines and practices.[11] Additionally, Dewey is most interested in children and adolescents where Foucault, although he uses children and the school in some of his examples, is more concerned with adults who are segregated in prisons, clinics, and hospitals.[12] But working focus aside, what is common to both is articulated by Dewey in the context of discussing experience's role in education. Dewey captures the centrality of habit in the formation of subjects, and thereby what interests us regarding the management of feelings, by saying that "The basic characteristic of habit is that every experience enacted and undergone modifies the one who acts and undergoes [it]."[13]

This is the heart of Foucault's view of habit formation and the construction of the self. The mechanism for constructing the self,

[9] Foucault 1979.
[10] Foucault 1979.
[11] Dewey, John, 1988, "Experience and Education." In Jo Ann Boydston, ed., 1988, *John Dewey: The Later Works, 1925–1953*, Vol. 13, Carbondale and Edwardsville: Southern Illinois University Press, 1–62.
[12] Foucault 1979.
[13] Dewey 1988, 18.

for shaping and reshaping persons, is the inculcation of habits that by being assimilated initially form and later partially reform the self, that shape and then reshape the person. The inculcation of habits is not the mere addition of habitual behavior, but is the alteration of the person because, as Dewey puts it in the foregoing passage, habits adopted result in behavior that in becoming the normal way for a person to act in various circumstances "modifies the one who acts." This is the Aristotelian insight: what we do often enough and for long enough eventually establishes not only what we do but ultimately who we are. In acquiring habits, emerging and existent subjects internalize their own actions and in this way habits are responsible for "the formation of attitudes."[14]

The coincidence of Foucault's views on discipline and Dewey's views on education, then, is that for both Foucault and Dewey the self is constructed, the person is formed, by self- and other-imposed habits. But more than this, the self is sustained by habits; essentially, the self as a self-reflective and social being is the sum of its habits. In a remark that could easily have been made by Foucault, Dewey tells us: "Were it not for the continued operation of all habits ... no such thing as character could exist." Character, he tells us, "is the interpenetration of habits."[15]

Children emulating their parents and peers as they grow and are socialized illustrates what Foucault and Dewey mean about character formation. Children's adoption of behavioral practices begins with unreflective, unintentional imitation of parents' and peers' verbal and nonverbal behavior. Unintentional imitation continues for a time, usually complemented and enhanced by partially or occasionally intentional mimicry prompted by the desire to be approved of and accepted. Eventually, both intentional and unintentional mimicry pass into unreflective habitual behavior, which comes to be simply the way the maturing children do things and, indirectly, the way they think. When the behavior reaches the stage of being habitual in the sense of being unthinking and automatic, when it has been internalized and assimilated, it is no longer self- or other-imposed but becomes what

[14] Dewey 1988, 19.
[15] Dewey, John, 1930, *Human Nature and Conduct: An Introduction to Social Psychology* (edition with new introduction by Dewey), New York: The Modern Library Dewey 1930, 38.

Foucault and Dewey understand to be the manifestation of personal character. As Dewey puts it, this process of adoption and eventual incorporation of practices is how "habits ... constitute the self."[16]

What we most need from Foucault is not his detailed treatment of the disciplinary processes that imbue habits. Clearly the time frames in which survivors must deal with electors' choices to die are much too short to rely on habit formation to get them through their ordeals. What we need from Foucault is appreciation of the very fact that habit formation functions as it does. That appreciation is a matter of coming to understand that the self, the subject, is a construct of behavior. That understanding then enables conception of the self as changeable through the very processes that first form it. We need the promise of self-redefinition, and that promise is present in Foucault's conception of the self as a malleable, ever-changing construct shaped and reshaped by self- and other-imposed habits.

The immediate relevance of Foucault's constructivist conception of the self to survivors' dealing with electors' decisions is how it facilitates comprehension that the feelings we have, even when prompted by the basic emotions of happiness, sadness, fear, anger, surprise, and disgust, are not all of them inexorable and predefined but are to a greater or lesser extent the results of conditioning and so are amenable to control and some measure of change. Too many people see sorrow and related affective responses to elective death as unavoidable reactions predetermined by an inviolate human nature. As a consequence, too many survivors see their affective responses to spouses', partners', relatives', or friends' choices to die as determinate realities that they have no choice but to accept or helplessly rail against. Contrary to this common view, survivors need to grasp that most of their feelings are amenable to change or management through what Foucault would describe as the application of discipline.

Recourse to Foucault's conception of the self, then, is a way to deal with the most basic issues posed by the first or conditional aspect of modifying the criterial approach to reasoning about elective death. The Foucauldian view of the self as constructed is intended to enable survivors to realize that they are adaptable in ways that not only

---

[16] Dewey 1930, 25.

allow them to control their feelings in order to cope rationally and effectively with electors' choices to die, but also to reshape themselves in ways that expedite their carrying on with their lives despite the elective deaths of their spouses, partners, relatives, or friends.

However, recognizing the possibility of control and adaptive change regarding the elective deaths of those close to them is only a start for survivors. To effectively control their feelings as well as to initiate successful longer-term adjustments to their new situations, survivors must first achieve a fairly significant degree of self-understanding regarding their affective reactions to electors' choices to die. This self-understanding is the core issue of the second aspect of modifying the criterial approach because self-understanding is a precondition of dealing as rationally and reasonably as is possible with electors' choices. The reason is that the biggest obstacle to productive coping with elective death is how education, personal history, and enculturation to a great extent determine how emotions or affective dispositions manifest themselves in feelings and are experienced by individuals. Survivors need to appreciate the extent to which what they feel is what they have been trained to feel and what they allow themselves to feel, and that neither is always what their emotions actually prompt.

Consider that even basic emotions, such as anger and fear, may be experienced by subjects as other than anger or fear. Short of full-fledged rage or terror, the feelings these emotions prompt are heavily conditioned by individuals' personal backgrounds and their established interpretive inclinations. The feelings internally presented to individuals who are, say, moderately angry or afraid are what training and enculturation determine to be felt, so the underlying emotions prompting the feelings may not be recognized for what they are. For instance, anger- and fear-prompted feelings often are experienced only as concern of one sort or another by the individuals who are angry or afraid. This is a phenomenon no doubt familiar to readers who are experienced medical ethicists or health-care practitioners and who have dealt with terminal patients, their relatives, and their friends.

It is fairly common in cases of elective death that what survivors feel is concern about electors and their decisions to die when the survivors actually are angry at electors and their decisions or fearful for themselves. What some survivors experience as concern for electors' well-being really may be anger at electors' preparedness to abandon relationships crucially important to survivors. Survivors may see electors as selfishly sacrificing too much time they might share for the sake of closure or because of self-serving or even cowardly unwillingness to endure their conditions a little longer. Again, self-directed anger at their own powerlessness, at their loss of control over electors' actions and situations, may be experienced by survivors as other-directed concern for those electors. Fear also may present itself as concern when potential survivors experience their fear of being left alone as concern about what their spouses or partners are doing in choosing to die.

An affective state that notoriously prompts feelings that masquerade as concern is guilt, and guilt masquerading as concern may prompt survivors to become seriously intrusive regarding electors' treatment and choices to die. The intrusiveness, which passes for making every effort to serve electors' best interests, will be prompted not by genuine concern for electors' well-being, but by suppressed self-reproach for previous neglect of electors or present failure to be adequately supportive of them and their decisions in their dire circumstances.

It is only when survivors are able to achieve self-reflective honesty about their feelings and the emotions prompting them that they can begin to think clearly about their affective states and how the products of those states may be influencing their perceptions of and reasoning about electors' choices to die. And only when that honesty is achieved can survivors begin the process of adapting themselves to their new realities. But achieving that honesty in the process of dealing with elective death may be quite difficult, requiring survivors to face and admit to themselves unwelcome truths about their emotional responses to electors' choices. Nonetheless, it is only when survivors genuinely understand their feelings and the emotions that prompt them that they can work toward preventing their feelings from negatively skewing their perceptions of and reasoning about electors' choices as well as toward averting psychological damage to themselves.

THE ROLE OF OTHERS

Survivors' inward reflection and efforts to be honest with themselves about their feelings regarding spouses', partners', relatives', and friends' decisions to die must be complemented by the input of others. This may seem unremarkable, but the reasons why others' input is necessary are complicated. The reasons center on how our emotional dispositions partly define us as persons, and therefore define us as the spouses, partners, relatives, and friends we are in relation to those closest to us. Survivors, then, are not just survivors or potential survivors of elective death; they are the complex persons they are, with all that entails about their emotional dispositions and the influences of those dispositions on their perceptions and reasoning as well as on how they continue their own lives after the elective deaths of their spouses, partners, relatives, and close friends.

The main complication necessitating the input of others is that as we saw above, survivors owe themselves respect for their self-defining emotional dispositions and they must take seriously the feelings that their emotions prompt, neither weakly succumbing to those feelings nor indiscriminately resisting them. This means that survivors must accommodate their feelings to a judiciously established degree in dealing with electors' choices to die. The problem is, of course, how survivors are to determine the degree of accommodation they may properly allow while preventing their feelings from distorting or counterproductively slanting their perceptions of and reasoning about electors' decisions to end their lives.

The complication posed by survivors' need to respect their own feelings and the emotions that prompt them is made significantly worse by how neither our emotions nor feelings are as well-defined as many seem to assume they are. This fact becomes evident as soon as individuals begin to reflect on their own feelings and the emotions that prompt them, and it becomes even clearer when others become involved in aiding them with their reflections. What emerges is that our feelings often are tentative and inchoate to a surprising degree, and a pivotal consequence of this is that unless we are dealing with fairly extreme instances of basic emotions, such as fear and anger – emotions that prompt quite definite feelings like terror and rage – reflection on our feelings tends to alter them to a significant extent.

This phenomenon further complicates elective-death survivors' efforts to understand and control their feelings regarding electors' decisions, and to make matters worse, it is not only the feeling-altering effects of self-reflection that pose difficulties. Feeling-altering effects are compounded by suggestion when others are involved in helping survivors reflect on their feelings.

Perhaps the most common way suggestion affects our feelings is when we try to voice how we feel about something to others, and find ourselves dissatisfied with and qualifying our self-attributions. Usually when this happens those to whom we are speaking offer descriptions that they think may better capture what we are trying to express. Sometimes this interaction can result in rather surprising reevaluations of our own feelings: reevaluations that alter or reshape what we are experiencing or thought we were experiencing. Let me clarify with two examples, both of which are personal in order to make my point more effectively than I might with concocted examples.

The first example has to do with how I felt anger at a former student for what I saw as him putting self-promotion ahead of integrity in his new job. Speaking to a colleague about the matter, I was surprised that I agreed with her when she told me that I was not angry but, rather, was disappointed in the former student, of whom I had thought better. An important aspect of this realization was me coming to understand that while I could have gotten over anger, disappointment was a deeper and more persistent attitudinal change because it carried with it negative reevaluation of the former student. My colleague's more apt description made clearer to me just how I was reacting to what I had learned about a person I thought I knew fairly well and had several times recommended on the basis of that initial impression.

The second example differs in that the feelings in question were not my own but those of a friend and it was I who offered the productive redescription. My friend spoke to me shortly after the death of someone we both had worked with occasionally for some years. My friend confessed that she felt guilty that our erstwhile colleague's death kept slipping from her mind and that she did not feel the loss more deeply. I pointed out that we had never been at all close to the individual in question and that she ought not to think that she must have deep feelings of loss just because we had sometimes worked together. I told her that I thought her reaction of obvious regret was sufficient and that no more was called for in the circumstances. I remember the look of surprise and relief on my friend's face when she faced what she had not been able to admit to herself, which was that she felt only conventional regret about our erstwhile colleague's death and acknowledged to herself that she really had no reason to feel more than that regret.

Both of these cases illustrate how another's contribution can better define one's own feelings, and definition of this sort often is necessary for effective reflection on one's feelings and the emotions that prompt them. However, both cases also raise the question whether when there is this sort of apparent improvement in individuals' self-awareness, we are dealing with differences made by genuine illumination and consequent clearer definition of feelings, or are dealing only with changes in feelings prompted by suggestion. A useful parallel can be drawn here with, of all things, indeterminacy in nuclear physics.

The point of the parallel is that in both cases, probing something alters what is probed. In physics, determining the position of a particle alters its velocity and determining its velocity alters its position; in dealing with human feelings, probing a feeling in an attempt to clarify it alters the feeling to some degree. Our affective states, unlike our physical states, are not as determinate as we often take them to be. Their determinacy seems to be a function of their strength, but even when feelings are very strong, they are not fixed and may quickly change or evaporate because of sudden realizations about their objects, distractions, mood changes, or others' interventions.

The first thing to note about how suggestion alters feelings is that it is not necessarily a bad thing for it to happen to survivors dealing with elective death. The overwhelming majority of survivors will be facing the elective death of a spouse, partner, family member, or close friend for the first time and lack experience in dealing with electors' choices. Survivors' feelings, then, initially will be confused and be so in ways usually prompting ambivalent and likely inappropriate responses to electors' choices. For instance, a quite common initial response on the part of survivors is dismissal of the idea that someone close to them seriously chooses to die. Usually survivors initially think that electors cannot really intend to end their lives and are only seeking reassurance, sympathy, or attention. If knowledgeable counselors effect changes in survivors' feelings through suggestion in such cases, so that survivors' feelings are more appropriate to the particular circumstances, that is all to the good despite the changes being effected through suggestion. Consultation with counselors may affect survivors' feelings through suggestion, but do so in a productive way by better defining and focusing their feelings. In fact, counselors and physicians normally try to alter survivors' feelings for their own good, and are usually concerned to get survivors to be more realistic about the situations they face.

Despite what some readers will likely think, it is misguided to respond to the foregoing by objecting that suggestion falsifies individuals' feelings, even though it admittedly may do so in practically beneficial ways. But feelings are not writ in stone; feelings are not true in some objective way, although vulnerable to being distortedly experienced or simply obscured because of suggestion. While emotions are underlying dispositional affective states, the feelings those states prompt are not anything independent of how they are experienced. If what is experienced changes, then feelings change. The emotions that prompt the feelings may persist as what they are, but if the feelings those emotions prompt change, there is no violation of something that was there before and persists though misperceived. In any case, suggestion does not always change feelings; sometimes suggestion only fills in gaps and resolves ambiguities. This often is precisely what those who counsel survivors attempt to achieve. Suggestion, then, can be a positive as well as a negative influence, and if suggestion is effected through the comments and advice of knowledgeable and perceptive counselors, it may significantly help survivors to better deal with electors' choices to die.

It is incontestable that our feelings color our perceptions and guide our reasoning. We are human, and regardless of how much we may aspire to embody the Aristotelian definition of human beings as rational animals, we are not wholly rational: our perceptions of and reasoning about ourselves, others, and events around us are conditioned by our affective states. We especially are not wholly rational in our actions and responses regarding anything that moves us deeply. But our inability to be wholly rational and objective in dealing with what we face is only part of how we fall short of the Aristotelian ideal.

The other part is that we do not know ourselves as well as we think we do. Our self-understanding, our self-awareness, is as much conditioned by our affective states as are our perceptions and reasoning.

Too often we are wrong about or even ignorant of our own beliefs and attitudes. For example, consider that there are any number of individuals who genuinely believe themselves to be open-minded and to be free of prejudices but who harbor prejudicial attitudes and have blinkered views of much they encounter. In the bulk of such cases individuals usually do not discover the nature of some of their beliefs and prejudices by their own efforts; usually they do so while interacting with others. For instance, they may say something that prompts questions or challenges because what they say is taken by interlocutors as racist or as implying racist views or as in some other way prejudicial. Such questions and challenges initially prompt denial by the speakers, but fortunately they sometimes also prompt productive reflection and consequent self-discovery about held beliefs and operant attitudes.

It is rather paradoxical that there is so much we think and believe that we do not realize we think and believe, and about which we rarely learn without the intervention of others. Contrary to what Descartes thought, our minds are not perfectly transparent to us – a fact on which psychiatrists and psychologists have based careers for many decades. However, what is of special concern to us here is that the opacity of much of what we think and believe plays an especially significant role in elective-death survivors' responses to electors' choices to die. Often only others can see how the influences of survivors' cognitive and affective states condition their perceptions of electors' decisions and how those influences may be skewing survivors' responses to those decisions. This is why internal reflection by itself is not enough when individuals are dealing with their spouses', partners', relatives', and friends' choices to die.

With respect to interventions by and the input of others, survivors have access to counseling of various sorts, from their simply talking with friends and relatives to consulting with professional counselors. As may be obvious, it is preferable that survivors consult professional, experienced counselors rather than rely only on relatives' and friends' suggestions and advice. However, what interests us at this point are not the sorts of counseling to which survivors might have recourse, but what survivors and lay and professional counselors must do to make counseling productive.

One clear requirement for productive counseling is that survivors' own reflections on their feelings need to be as frank and uncompromising as possible in order to provide reliable bases for effective counseling. A second clear requirement is that once counseling has begun, survivors' own reflections need to be monitored by those providing counseling and who often can achieve greater perspicacity and objectivity regarding survivors' feelings and perceptions of the situations with which they must deal. A third requirement is even more demanding: counselors, especially lay counselors, must maintain a difficult balance between commiserating with survivors and objectively assessing their responses to electors' choices to die.

This third requirement is complicated by how counselors must not only be judicious and objective about survivors' perceptions and reasoning, but also about how they themselves are construing the situations that survivors face. In particular, counselors must take into account cultural influences on both survivors and themselves; they need to be clear on how cultural influences may be affecting survivors' perceptions and reasoning, as well as how similar or different cultural influences may be affecting their own perceptions and reasoning and therefore the counsel they offer to survivors. Otherwise, cultural influences may play a decisive part in either prompting too-ready endorsement of electors' decisions or obstructing fair assessment and acceptance of those decisions by disallowing or preempting various considerations.

As I have been maintaining, survivors' assessments of electors' reasoning and motivation are greatly complicated by the need to give due weight to their own feelings while at the same time guarding against the distortions those feelings may and often do cause. Survivors giving due weight to their own feelings in assessing their spouses', partners', relatives', and friends' choices to die is a function of what I spoke of in Chapter 1 as survivors having a personal stake in electors' well-being. In a close relationship, the well-being and best interests of each party cannot be considered in isolation; the interests and well-being of each bear directly on the interests and well-being of the other. This is clearest in the case of spouses and partners, especially those whose relationships are of significant duration. For this reason, in the balance of this chapter I will focus on spouses and partners in order to capture the interdependency of interests in the most intimate relationships. It then will be easier to generalize and extrapolate to relationships that in different ways approximate the intimacy of spouses and partners, but which usually involve lesser degrees of closeness in varying respects.

To reiterate, elective-death survivors assessing their spouses' and partners' choices to die face the difficult task of understanding and assessing their reasoning and motivation while at the same time considering how the choices affect their own interests and well-being. The most serious problems with doing so arise when survivors in one or another way, consciously or unconsciously, are unwilling to accept the loss incurred by spouses' and partners' deaths. The striking thing is that this unwillingness may occur even if survivors share spouses' or partners' perceptions of their circumstances and prospects as hopeless and survivors appreciate that their spouses and partners clinging to life harms them more than does abandoning life.

Survivors' unwillingness or at least reluctance to accept the loss of spouses and partners manifests itself in different forms. One of these forms is psychological denial of one or another kind, but this particular form of reluctance or unwillingness lies beyond the scope of this book. Another form is rationalizations that are basically self-serving interpretations and that are imposed on spouses' and partners' elective-death reasons and motives. One instance of this sort of rationalization has survivors construing their spouses' or partners' decisions to abandon life by deliberate choice as basically selfish unpreparedness to bear a certain amount of suffering for the sake of more time together. This particular form of rationalization is fairly extreme, but it has a milder and very much more common variant.

As anticipated in the previous chapter, the most familiar manifestation of rationalized unwillingness to accept spouses' and partners' elective-death decisions is seeing their decisions as too hasty. What is mainly operant in this reaction is that survivors' time frames for spouses' or partners' acceptable elective deaths invariably are of considerably greater duration than spouses' and partners' own time frames. They are so partly as a function of survivors' persistent hopes for even transient improvements in electors' circumstances, and partly as a function of suppressed expectations that spouses or partners will tolerate suffering for a longer time for the sake of remaining together.

Unwillingness to accept electors' decisions, of course, manifests itself in various other ways of resisting or rejecting those decisions, and most of them show how survivors' reason and emotions can be mixed in ways that foster contrary and even contradictory feelings about electors' choices and enactment of those choices. Often what is most evident, both to survivors and those trying to help them, is persistent ambivalence. Survivors may voice acceptance of electors' choices on some occasions, only to voice rejection or denial of them on other occasions. On the former sort of occasion, survivors often aver and apparently genuinely believe that they now have made up their minds, that they now have accepted electors' decisions, but then they reverse themselves hours or even minutes later. However, difficulty of acceptance is not all that survivors and those counseling them have to worry about. In some cases survivors may succeed too well in reasoning their way to acceptance of electors' decisions but may then be plagued for years and even the rest of their lives for not having trusted their feelings regarding spouses' or partners' choices to die, feeling that it would have been more honest for them to renounce electors' decisions than to go along with those decisions on the basis of reasoning. This outcome is especially likely with respect to spouses and partners, but it is also probable with respect to relatives and friends where the relationships are particularly close or where there is a high degree of emotional dependency on the part of survivors. It also may be that the dependency obstructing acceptance is wholly practical.[17]

Survivors' unwillingness to accept electors' choices and how their unwillingness manifests itself make clear that as in most cases, there are discrepancies between what individuals think and feel, and that these discrepancies often are neither properly understood nor adequately resolved. We need to look more closely at how reasoning and feelings work and affect one another in determining attitudes toward and judgments about situations survivors face. As will emerge, the crucial point is how survivors initially construe those situations.

---

[17] I was told by one of the several medical people I have spoken to that the elderly spouse of a patient who opted to cease treatment, when told of the decision, immediately said: "But who'll drive me to my appointments?"

In October 2008, the *New York Times* carried an article regarding the economic crisis that so disrupted peoples' lives in the Fall of that year. The article focused on financial decisions, but in the process of proposing that some elements of currently accepted understanding of how we make decisions need to be revised, the article provides an admirably succinct recapitulation of how we generally make decisions. Although it was in the public media rather than a learned journal, the article offers something of major significance to our concerns and does so in a clear and compelling way. What the article highlights as needing rethinking about decision making is a factor that plays a key role in how survivors perceive and reason about electors' choices to die.

The article begins by pointing out that "there are four steps to every decision. First, you perceive a situation. Then you think of possible courses of action. Then you calculate which course is in your best interest. Then you take the [indicated] action." The article's main point, and what is of greatest interest to us, is that though calculating what action is in one's best interests has traditionally been thought to be the most important step in decision making, the intricacies of the credit collapse in the Fall of 2008 showed that we need to "shift our focus from step three, rational calculation, to step one, perception." The author notes that "[p]erceiving a situation seems, at first glimpse, like a remarkably simple operation.... But the operation that seems most simple is actually the most complex."[18]

The reason given for the complexity is of great significance to our concerns. As presented in the article, the reason is that in perceiving situations, most of what is involved in shaping perceptions "takes place below the level of awareness." Most important, there is an interplay of biases that escape conscious reflection. The article considers the kinds of biases that unconsciously distort our perceptions and hones in on the one that is of special interest to us: "our tendency to see data that confirm our prejudices more vividly than data that contradict them."[19]

We seem to be naturally inclined to be more impressed by observations that confirm our views and expectations than by observations

[18] Brooks, David, 2008, "The Behavioral Revolution," *New York Times*, Oct. 28, A23.
[19] Brooks 2008, A23.

that run counter to those views and expectations. We give greater weight to what we observe when it agrees with our beliefs and values than when it does not. Consider an example of this disposition, or what we can call our preferential-weighting inclination, and how it works in the area that concerns us. In assessing electors' choices to die, survivors will be inclined to take hopeful prognoses as more compelling than less hopeful ones. There will be various reasons for survivors to do so, but we can readily formulate a specific one as being that the hopeful prognoses coincide with survivors' own emotional resistance to there being sufficient cause for electors' to choose to die.

In most cases, survivors will have little by way of solid grounds to favor an optimistic prognosis over more pessimistic ones; most probably they will rely only on what they are told by physicians or others caring for their spouses, partners, relatives, or friends. Survivors may not even compare what they are told with what electors are told or may discount what electors are told. Possibly survivors will prefer not to know if the prognoses they themselves have been given are merely routine reassurances by physicians or other health-care professionals and not intended to be their considered opinions. More likely is that survivors will interpret prognoses as more hopeful than physicians intend them to be. For example, survivors may automatically focus on the longest survival period those physicians offer in describing electors' best and worst chances, or fasten on the most optimistic of the highest and lowest possibilities regarding efficacy of treatment.

However accomplished and manifested, survivors' preferential inclinations can distort how they perceive electors' situations and unduly underestimate the reality of electors' levels of suffering, emotional exhaustion, and pressing desire to see an end to pain and continuing deterioration. But preferential-weighting inclination also may work the other way by unduly strengthening support for electors' decisions. For instance, if survivors incline to believe that it is in electors' best interests to end their suffering, exhaustion, and inescapable decline, survivors could disproportionately discount genuinely optimistic prognoses and support or even encourage choices to die that are, in fact, premature.

Whether our preferential-weighting inclination questionably disposes survivors to support or obstruct electors' decisions is a function of how survivors' values and beliefs structure their perceptions of electors' circumstances, prospects, and options. However, recognizing this reality does not take us very far regarding survivors' responses to elective death. For one thing, trying to anticipate the effects of preferential-weighting inclinations on survivors' thinking is seriously hampered by how, for the majority of them, involvement with elective death is not only greatly disturbing but most commonly is a new experience. This means that experience-based anticipation on the part of both survivors and those counseling them regarding how preferential weighting will shape and color survivors' perceptions is unreliable. For example, it often is the case that individuals who previously considered themselves broadminded and liberal regarding elective death find that when it affects them directly they cannot condone choices to die. Further complicating anticipation of survivors' perceptions is that they may vary considerably depending on who it is that chooses to die. Most individuals likely would be more tolerant of elective-death decisions made by relatives or friends than by spouses or partners, but the reverse of this may be true; greater intimacy might support acceptance because of survivors' better understanding of the suffering being endured by their partners or spouses. Knowing that preferential weighting conditions survivors' perceptions, then, serves us more as a caution than as a basis for anticipating how they perceive elective-death choices made by their spouses or partners, their relatives or friends.

REASONING BASICS

We now need to review some basics about reasoning in order to better understand how preferential weighting may misdirect survivors' reasoning about electors' choices by biasing how they construe the objects of their reasoning. Most fundamental for our purposes is that while some reasoning is abstract or speculative, it is practical reasoning that is relevant here because our concern is with what elective-death survivors do in response to electors' choices to die. The first point is that practical reasoning is purposive; it is directed on resolving issues to the best extent possible in order to enable acting in the most rational and productive way possible given one's aims and intentions.

The second point is that practical reasoning operates on data possessed: long-held or newly acquired beliefs and information about the various aspects, particulars, and parameters of what is being reasoned about and what is known and can be reasonably predicted about the courses of action being considered. Unfortunately, the data possessed or acquired is seldom complete and/or certain. In the case of survivors, a significant part of the data on the basis of which they must reason is prognostic; additionally, another significant part is about electors' states of mind, which are only inferentially accessible. Survivors' reasoning, therefore, must proceed like much practical reasoning: on the basis of the preponderance of evidence supporting the data available and on survivors' best approximations of electors' states of mind. A compound consequence of both of these considerations is that preferential weighting may play a major if not decisive role in survivors' reasoning by inclining survivors to assess available evidence and approximate electors' states of mind too much in line with their own preferences and expectations.

Survivors' reasoning about electors' choices, if it is to be sound, requires that they identify their interpretive inclinations in order to appreciate and assess the extent to which preferential weighting may be affecting their thinking. The most meticulous reasoning about electors' choices will prove counterproductive if it is targeted on misperceived situations. For example, survivors may misguidedly perceive electors' choices to die as prompted by abhorrence of being burdens or by depression instead of by no longer bearable suffering and well-grounded recognition of the hopelessness of their situations. Such misperceptions likely are determined by survivors' affective resistance to recognizing that elective death is in electors' best interests and how preferential weighting emphasizes positive factors and occludes negative ones in electors' prognoses and personal accounts of their conditions. But as the article referred to above discusses, the problem is that preferential weighting operates below the level of reflective awareness. Its results are distorted perceptions, but it is those perceptions that are the immediate contents of survivors' consciousness, not the weighting that shapes them.

How, then, can survivors guard against preferential weighting and reason soundly about electors' choices? In *Choosing to Die*, I stressed the need for electors to discuss their reasoning, motivation, and decisions with others who are able to provide different perspectives on their choices to die, emphasizing the need for cross-cultural input. In that book the primary aim was achieving the soundest and most balanced possible assessment of electors' own reasoning and motivation; in this book our concern is with survivors' perceptions of and reasoning about electors' choices to die. The soundest and most balanced possible assessment is still the aim, but the difference here is the need to factor in survivors' own feelings into the assessments of their perceptions and reasoning about electors' decisions. The main problem this need poses is that while reasoning can be tested for errors, such as using beliefs as established facts in premises and invalidly drawing conclusions on that basis, it is difficult to insure that survivors' construals of the situations they reason about are not distorted by misperceptions. The only way for survivors to achieve the necessary degree of objectivity to insure the soundness of their reasoning is to involve others in their deliberations in order to avail themselves of different perspectives on both the situations they face and their construals of those situations.

The involvement of others in electors' or survivors' thinking about elective death is not a matter of those others, be they professionals or laypersons, providing authoritative assessments. A reviewer of *Choosing to Die* missed this key point of my proposal regarding electors' use of the input of others.[20] The reviewer read the proposal as if I were claiming special insight and primacy for the viewpoints of others. This was neither what I intended nor what is described in the book. My point was that the proffering of others' perspectives on elective-death decisions enabled electors to reflect more efficaciously on their reasoning and motivation. Similarly, in the present context the proposal is that the proffering of others' perspectives enables survivors to better reflect on and understand their own perceptions and reasoning regarding electors' choices to die.

The proffering of others' perspectives initially works by simply providing alternatives to electors' and survivors' own perspectives on elective death. The point is that the alternatives effectively pose implicit and often explicit questions about electors' and survivors'

---

[20] Young 2008.

perspectives and how they are applying their perspectives in considering their own or their spouses', partners', relatives', or friends' elective-death decisions. Once questions are posed by the sheer availability of alternative perspectives, further input from others can greatly facilitate achievement of objectivity in electors' and survivors' reflections. In the case of survivors, which is our present concern, input from others also serves to maintain their awareness of how the elective-death choices they are assessing are, after all, choices made by others: others with their own perspectives, even if survivors share intimate relationships with them. It is counterproductive for survivors to identify too closely with electors' situations and choices.

CHAPTER SUMMARY

The objective in this chapter was to get clearer on the more important ways in which affective states influence survivors' responses to spouses' and partners', relatives' and friends' elective-death choices. The main focus was how emotion-prompted feelings affect survivors' reasoning about electors' decisions and need to be managed, but two subsidiary focal points quickly arose. The first had to do with how it is possible to manage emotion-prompted feelings; the second had to do with the role of our preferential-weighting inclinations and how they tend to distort survivors' perceptions of events and assessments of information available to them about electors' situations and prospects and their reasoning and motives.

With respect to feelings' influences, the most important thing is to recognize that feelings do influence perception and reasoning and need to be controlled. With respect to controlling feelings, we had recourse to Foucault's constructivist understanding of the self and his and Dewey's insights into inculcation of habits as defining and redefining the self. The aim was to show that feelings are not the inevitable and determinate products of a "human nature" and are amenable to management and even change through self- or other-imposed discipline or retraining.

However, controlling feelings and their influences to proper and desired ends presupposes being clear on their objects, and it emerged that one of the most troublesome aspects of reasoning about elective death is misconstruing what is reasoned about because of preferential weighting of the information available. For example, electors in dire and hopeless circumstances may be misperceived as having a significant chance of improvement in their conditions because of preferential weighting given select elements of their prognoses.

In the next chapter we need to look more closely at how culture affects reasoning about elective death; we also must begin to formulate a workable criterion or set of criteria to equip survivors to better and more consistently assess electors' choices to die as well as to better understand the consequences to themselves of spouses, partners, relatives, or friends surrendering their lives and their relationships to escape extended and irremediable mental and physical suffering.

3

Culture's Elusive Role

There are two sorts of cultures the components of which influence electors' reasoning and motivation regarding elective death and survivors' perceptions and assessments of electors' choices to die. The familiar sort is made up of what I called "iconic" cultures in *Choosing to Die*. These are the interwoven ethnic, regional, and religious values, the social behavioral standards and familial structures, and the ritualistic observances and day-to-day practices that we collectively describe as "Western European culture," "Asian culture," "Hispanic culture," and the like.[1] The less familiar sort of culture is made up of what I dubbed "coincidental" cultures in *Choosing to Die*.[2] These are interwoven sets of values, standards, and practices, as are iconic cultures, but coincidental cultures differ from iconic ones because they arise not from ethnic or religious roots or historical circumstances, but from people coming together in pursuit of a common objective. This is why coincidental cultures usually cut across iconic boundaries in that their members often are members of diverse iconic cultures.

Coincidental cultures may and do arise wholly within iconic cultures, with all their members sharing the same iconic values, standards, and practices in addition to coincidental ones. The most evident cases of intra-iconic coincidental cultures are those shared

[1] Sack, Kevin. 2008, "Doctors Miss Cultural Needs, Study Says," *New York Times*, Tuesday, June 10, 2008, 12.
[2] Prado 2008, 180, 186.

by members of groups who share particularly strict or extreme interpretations of their common iconic cultures, and who are united primarily by their zeal to defend and propagate their interpretations. However, coincidental cultures internal to particular iconic cultures are not of immediate relevance to our concerns since our main interest is in disparities and conflicts between iconic and coincidental cultures, not interpretive disputes within iconic cultures.

Though partly regional in a sense that has to do with the particular location of interaction, coincidental cultures are primarily defined by particular activities: activities that may span considerable periods of time, as in the case of professions, or that are more temporally limited, as in the case of *ad hoc* working groups. More specifically, coincidental cultures are engendered by common interests and especially by objectives, as noted above, and by the values and practices generated by those interests and objectives. Coincidental cultures do not arise only from activities purposely entered into; they also arise from reactive joint efforts to deal with particular features of members' environments or of the areas of interactive activity – for instance, specific dangers, communal challenges, deprivations, and even certain abundances.

The paradigm case of a coincidental culture is the ethos of the workplace, where people of varying iconic cultural backgrounds work together to achieve shared collective and personal goals by engaging in formally and informally stipulated activities and adhering to formally and informally stipulated rules of conduct. Another paradigmatic instance of a coincidental culture is less obvious, but one that involves surprisingly strict standards and rules of conduct: the ethos of the urban neighborhood. With respect to paradigms, though, the example that most clearly illustrates the nature of coincidental cultures, mainly because it is the one most readily recognized by the majority of people, is the ethos of the military. Members of armies and their several subsections – divisions, brigades, companies, platoons, and squads – develop shared values and practices as do people in a workplace, but they also develop strong loyalties to their respective units or groups and acquire striking recognitional capacities regarding their fellows. Additionally, the range of sections and subsections in armies brings out how loyalties developed in coincidental cultures tend to increase in strength as group memberships decrease in numbers.

For our purposes, the essential point about coincidental cultures is that their members share values and practices that may conflict with and override their iconic cultural values and practices. For example, think of two groups of individuals, one group whose members share a Western European Christian iconic cultural background, and one group whose members share a Middle Eastern Muslim iconic cultural background. Now think of both groups living in the same urban neighborhood and have the members of the two groups be similarly employed and in the same upscale economic class. Both groups will share a common coincidental culture determined by their circumstances and despite their iconic cultural differences. As a consequence, members of each iconic group will have more common interests and objectives with members of the other iconic group than with other members of their respective iconic cultures who live in different neighborhoods, are differently employed or unemployed, and are in a less privileged economic class. It is virtually inevitable that some of the coincidental cultural values and practices of the members of these two groups will override their iconic ones, especially in day-to-day situations in which specific challenges to cultural affiliations do not arise or at least not in serious ways.

It is the possible variance in how iconic and coincidental cultures influence individuals that introduces significant complications with respect to survivors' perceptions of and reasoning about electors' decisions. This possible variance roughly doubles the number of factors survivors and those counseling them need to consider in assessing their responses to electors' choices to die because survivors' perceptions and reasoning are influenced by both their iconic and their coincidental cultural values and practices. However, there is still more involved regarding cultural influences.

First, it is increasingly the case in our multicultural society that spouses and partners have different iconic cultural backgrounds, as they most likely have different coincidental cultures. Second, although survivors and their relatives who choose to die will normally share the same iconic cultural background, their coincidental cultures very probably will differ. Third, despite the fact that most people befriend those with whom they work or have a good deal in common, the iconic and coincidental cultures of survivors and some of their friends who choose to die will differ. Fourth, even where survivors and electors share iconic and coincidental cultures, there may be differences in their personal interpretations of cultural values, requirements, and prohibitions. This is particularly true given contemporary interpretive tolerances. Fifth, survivors and those counseling them may have different iconic cultural backgrounds and almost certainly will have different coincidental cultures. Sixth, survivors' perceptions and reasoning also may be influenced to a greater or lesser extent by the iconic and coincidental cultural values of the physicians and other professionals caring for electors. One way in which this latter sort of influence commonly occurs is through survivors encountering and being affected by what is no doubt familiar to some readers, which is the variety of more and less permissive attitudes toward elective death shown by physicians and other health-care professionals.

All of this means that survivors may be influenced not only by their own iconic and coincidental values but also in some measure by the iconic and coincidental cultural values of their spouses, partners, relatives, and close friends who choose to die, as well as of their counselors and those caring for electors. And as if all of the foregoing complications were not enough, perhaps the most serious problem regarding consideration of cultural influences on survivors has to do with recognition of the iconic cultural values operant in the influencing of survivors' perceptions and reasoning. The root of the problem is straightforward ignorance rather than bias or prejudice, as might be assumed. Members of iconic cultures are aware of iconic cultures other than their own, and of there being significant differences among them. The majority are inclined to respect those differences to some degree, but the trouble is that their knowledge of how other iconic cultures differ from their own commonly is limited to a small number of obvious factors: diversity in language, religion, and dress, and often marital practices and notable dietary restrictions.

With respect to elective death, awareness of and attention to possibly influentially active iconic cultural values are nearly exclusively focused on elements that are familiar because of media attention to or common talk about cultural differences. Of these the most familiar is cultural prohibition of suicide or elective death, and often many

complexities in survivors' responses to electors' choices are misguidedly glossed as their inability to reconcile electors' choices with this
one widely shared cultural prohibition. As we might expect, the
problem of ignorance is much greater with respect to coincidental
cultures, where the only value that is usually obvious to nonmembers
is members' group loyalty.

What makes the ignorance problem regarding iconic cultures
more or less endemic is the sad reality that most people first become
aware of iconic cultural differences as children but do so in deplorably
negative ways. Young children first have to learn to recognize iconic
cultural differences as characterizing groups rather than as characteristic only of particular individuals they encounter. Unfortunately,
they usually learn this lesson in two ultimately counterproductive
ways: by hearing jokes made by adults and older playmates about
members of other iconic cultures, and through parental exclusionary
cautions or prohibitions concerning potential playmates belonging
to other iconic cultures. Few children have escaped being warned not
to play with the children of "those people" in their neighborhoods,
and fewer still have never heard adults or older children make jokes
disparaging members of other cultures.

One of the worst consequences of learning about cultural differences through disparaging jokes and discriminatory prohibitions is
that the cultures so identified become objectified in ways that impede,
if they do not altogether preclude, the affected children later taking
those cultures seriously when they become adults. Attitudes learned
and assimilated at an early age require conscious and determined
effort to be reversed or set aside in later years, and initiating such
effort usually requires persuasive reasons that may only rarely arise.
Moreover, unfortunate attitudes adopted in childhood toward some
cultures tend to color and spill over to attitudes adopted toward other
cultures encountered or learned about in adulthood.

With such inauspicious beginnings being the rule rather than the
exception, it is no surprise that our collective contemporary response
to multiculturalism is normally couched in terms of tolerance rather
than in more positive terms of embracement. Many seem to think
that the reason for emphasis on tolerance is because of something
like a natural xenophobia, and there may be a good deal of truth
in the idea that the normal human inclination, like the normal

animal inclination, is to shun the different, the unfamiliar. It would be interesting, however, to see how an absence of disparaging jokes and exclusionary prohibitions would affect a generation or two of children.

In any case, the present reality is that general awareness of iconic cultural diversity, while improving, falls markedly short of the levels of knowledge needed to facilitate identification of iconic cultural influences on survivors' perceptions and reasoning regarding electors' choices to die. Additionally, there is far too little recognition of coincidental cultures and therefore of their influence to allow ready identification of how they affect survivors. In short, cultural influences on survivors pose serious difficulties with respect to understanding how survivors are affected by them in dealing with electors' choices. Unfortunately, this is not a problem we can solve here or even consider in the detail it merits. What we can and need to do is to focus on the aspect of the problem that is particularly relevant to our concerns and discussion of which falls within the limits of this book.

The most important aspect of how both iconic and coincidental cultures influence survivors' perceptions of and reasoning about electors' choices to die is how the two sorts of enculturation determine, if not emotions themselves, then how emotions are manifested and how they are subjectively experienced as feelings. To understand the importance of this it must be appreciated that little of what is felt by individuals is either simple or has simple causes. Most of what we feel is a complex product of stimulated affective dispositions and acquired and developed conditioning factors. Little that we feel is just what it seems; as has been noted, it is only in extreme cases of basic emotions like fear and anger that we feel in direct or unconditioned ways what these emotions prompt.

Another aspect of how iconic and coincidental cultural influences affect survivors' thinking, an aspect of only somewhat lesser importance, is a version of what we encountered in connection with religious beliefs in reasoning about elective death, and is that iconic and coincidental enculturation engenders beliefs that, like religious ones, may be used by survivors as facts in reasoning about electors' choices to die. Cultural beliefs functioning as facts in the reasoning that determines survivors' attitudes toward electors' choices jeopardizes the soundness of survivors' responses to those choices. However, although this latter is a major issue and merits serious attention, we need to address the more pressing issue of which emotions actually are influentially operant when survivors experience certain feelings in responding to electors' choices. It is of crucial importance that survivors understand that their feelings are not always accurate manifestations of their active emotions, and that iconic and coincidental cultural influences play a major role in determining what feelings they experience when their emotions are stimulated.

FEELINGS' CAUSES AND INFLUENCES

With respect to how enculturation shapes the way feelings are experienced, and thereby how it may to some extent obscure the emotions that prompt the feelings, consider as an example how in a given culture anger might be tightly controlled and redirected. In such a case, cultural conditioning could result in individuals construing the feelings prompted by anger falling short of rage as, say, temptations or provocations regarding self-control. Such construal of feelings prompted by anger is initially a learned response, but when it occurs often enough construal becomes experience in the sense that the anger actually comes to be felt differently. What happens is that feelings of anger toward the causes of the anger – toward whatever stimulated the emotion – come to be experienced as feelings of self-reproach and embarrassment. The process that results in this shift is that the feelings the emotion initially prompts are objectified through training as somehow improper and belittling and as having more to do with challenging internal self-mastery than with whatever prompted them. From individuals' internal perspectives in the process of enculturation, it will seem that they are discovering something about their feelings in construing feelings of anger as provocations or temptations when what is really happening is that enculturation is changing what they feel when anger is provoked in them.

Some readers may think at this point that too much is being attributed to enculturation. This, however, is a shortsighted view. It is, in fact, difficult to overestimate the effects of enculturation. We must remember that the process is a holistic one, that no aspect of our lives is untouched by enculturation. "We become cultured through training in various activities, such as customs, arts, ways of interacting with people, and the use of technologies, and the learning of ideas, beliefs, shared philosophies, and religion."[3] This leaves little of our daily lives unaffected. Consider language. The most extensive aspect of enculturation is the linguistic. Before learning customs and technologies we learn our native languages, and in our doing so many facets of how we experience the world are so profoundly established that few ever realize that they are not totally natural. Research has shown, for instance, that a "Japanese six-month-old can hear the English *r-l* distinction as well as an American infant. At one year she no longer can."[4] Children learning Japanese as their first language lose the ability to distinguish between two verbal sounds that other children readily differentiate. But more than this, as a result of the nature of their most basic level of enculturation, they lack an auditory capacity they are unaware they have lost or ever had. Nor is this sort of phenomenon limited to language and auditory capacities; visual and manipulative capacities are similarly affected.[5]

The process of learned construals of feelings being assimilated and thus reshaping what individuals experience takes us back to our discussion of habit formation in Chapter 2. There our concern was to understand how persons are formed by what they do, rather than what they do being determined by what they are. The heart of our consideration of habit formation in Chapter 2 was Aristotle's understanding of how repeated behavior is assimilated and establishes how individuals think and act. It was this understanding on which Foucault and Dewey built to develop their views of discipline and education. Here our concern is more narrowly focused on how what emotions prompt in us may come to be experienced in ways determined by enculturation. The relevance to survivors' responses to electors' choices to die is obvious: enculturation affects their responses to the extent that it determines what they feel in being presented with electors' choices. Therefore, consideration of survivors' responses to their spouses,

[3] Doidge, Norman, 2007, *The Brain That Changes Itself.* New York: Penguin Books, 287.
[4] Kuhl, Patricia, Barbara T. Conboy, Sharon Coffey-Corina, Dennis Padden, Maritza Rivera-Gaxiola, and Tobey Nelson, 2008, "Phonetic Learning as a Pathway to Language: New Data and Native Language Magnet Theory Expanded (NLM-e)," *Philosophical Transactions of the Royal Society B*, 2008, 363, 979–1000.
[5] Doidge 2007, 289–91.

partners, relatives, or friends opting for elective death must take into account that what they feel may not accurately reflect the emotions they actually are having.

Our feelings are not inviolate experiential effects of our emotions; they are open to slanting that misrepresents their causes. We must remember that "[c]ulture is not just produced by the brain; it is also by definition a series of activities that shape the mind."[6] How we are reared and enculturated has a great deal to do with how we feel what we feel and with what we allow ourselves to feel, and what we allow ourselves to feel in some cases may be different from what the emotions we are having would prompt us to feel if enculturated responses did not intervene.

Note that in the passage just quoted it appears that the brain and mind are uncritically glossed, but this is neither careless thinking nor writing. An identification of the mind and brain, the mental and the neurophysiological, is implicit in what has been said earlier and in the Foreword about emotions as dispositional bodily states and feelings as what we experience of emotions or those bodily states. Up to now it would be possible, for ontological reasons, to interpret our consideration of feelings and emotions in terms of some dualistic understanding of the relation of mind and body. However, doing so becomes much more difficult when we consider how enculturation shapes what we feel when our emotions are stimulated. In *The Brain That Changes Itself,* Norman Doidge offers an account of the processes by which culture conditions brain activity and thereby how it conditions the mind or the way we think.[7] In arguing as he does, Doidge leaves little room for thinking of the mind and brain as two different substances related only by some kind of one-way causal connection.

The basis of Doidge's contentions about culture and the brain is his endorsement of what he and others call "neuroplasticity": a view of the brain/mind as able to reorganize itself in the sense that areas such as the occipital cortex, previously considered to be limited to vision, might acquire new functions, such as hearing, through a complex process combining natural responses and purposive training. Although

[6] Doidge 2007, 287.
[7] Doidge 2007.

Doidge's book is a popular one – the *New York Times* describes it as straddling "the gap between science and self-help" – the research he draws on is serious enough and so his book is of real value to us.[8]

Basing his contentions on recent research and his own experience as a psychiatrist, psychoanalyst, and researcher, Doidge challenges the accepted view of the brain as hardwired for its various functions, contending that "[n]europlastic research has shown us that every sustained activity ever mapped – including physical activities, sensory activities, learning, thinking, and imagining – changes the brain as well as the mind."[9] What interests us about Doidge's contentions is not only that he considers areas of the brain capable of acquiring new functions, but that he does not consider that it does so only through natural processes, such as other senses becoming more acute if one is lost, as when deafness results in heightened peripheral vision.[10] What is of relevance to our concerns in Doidge's contentions is his view of the brain as also changing through self- and other-imposed behavioral activity, and what is of greatest import in this is that cultural activities "are no exception. Our brains are modified by the cultural activities we do."[11]

The body of Doidge's book mainly is about individual cases of people who retrained their brains and themselves. The material that concerns us is presented in an appendix titled "The Culturally Modified Brain."[12] There Doidge maintains that "[c]ultural differences are ... persistent because when our native culture is learned and wired into our brains, it becomes 'second nature', seemingly as 'natural' as many of the instincts we were born with."[13] It is this idea that enculturation is a "wiring" into our brains of values and practices that best explains how enculturation affects and to a great extent determines how we experience what our dispositional affective states, our emotions, cause us to feel. Doidge's presentation of how enculturation works essentially is a contemporary and scientifically informed expression of the Aristotelian view of habit formation

---

[8] Doidge 2007, front cover.
[9] Doidge 2007, 288.
[10] Doidge 2007, 295–96.
[11] Doidge 2007, 288.
[12] Doidge 2007, 288–311.
[13] Doidge 2007, 299.

and its consequences, and as such it amplifies the core of Foucault and Dewey's views on discipline and education. In this way, Doidge's presentation lends scientific detail and weight to what I say earlier about how iconic and coincidental cultures influence survivors' perceptions and reasoning.

However, Doidge's work and the research he relies on only explain how enculturation changes us and that it can alter the ways we actually feel what our emotions prompt. In this, Doidge supports Foucault and Dewey, but he takes us no farther than they do. The main reason I have recourse to Doidge is to show that there is actively ongoing scientific work on the effects of enculturation. But that done, we need to consider the more abstract aspect of how habit in general and enculturation in particular establish much of what we feel in shaping us as subjects and so as persons, and doing so comes down to acknowledging a fundamental Kantian point. Fortunately, although this Kantian point was revolutionary when it was first made, it has long since become a fundamental element in our understanding of ourselves, of cognition, and of sensory awareness, so it needs little more than restating here.

The essence of the matter is that there is no such thing as raw awareness. Everything of which we become aware is conceptualized in the process of becoming an object of awareness. Everything of which we are aware must be conceptualized for us to be aware of it. We never see, hear, feel, taste, or smell just what is there; we always see, hear, feel, taste, or smell something as objectified by our concepts. Even when we are aware of something that puzzles us, something that we cannot immediately identify, we are aware of it under some description and that is to say we conceptualize it. Moreover, this is as true about our feelings as it is about things we perceive in the world, which is why the Kantian point is important to our concerns: what we feel, like what we perceive, is conceptualized. Once we pass the stage at which we are infants unthinkingly reacting to stimuli, once we acquire self-consciousness and self-reflection, what we experience of our stimulated dispositional affective states is conceptualized by us as particular feelings.

The distinction drawn in the Foreword and earlier between emotions and feelings facilitates understanding the Kantian point's application to what we experience of our emotions. We have emotions, and emotions are stimulated in us by all sorts of things and events. But emotions are dispositional bodily states, and when they are stimulated or activated, they are ongoing bodily events that are not necessarily experienced. When we do experience our emotions is when they cause feelings, and as just noted, our feelings are like all our other perceptions in the sense that they are conceptualized in becoming objects of awareness. When a given emotion is stimulated in us we experience what it causes in us as a particular feeling that is shaped by numerous factors in our personal histories, some of which are peculiar to us and some of which are cultural. This is less true of extreme cases of the basic emotions, especially fear, but in those cases what we feel invariably follows immediate, unthought reactions like crying out or taking flight.

We can pull together some of the foregoing in this way: everything of which we are aware is conceptualized. Some concepts, like some emotions, are basic, are givens; as fear and anger are basic emotions, our conceptualizations of temporality, individuality, and cause-effect are basic to our mode of consciousness. But the majority of concepts are acquired, learned, and must be knowingly applied at first. In a similar way, many of the ways we feel when our emotions are acquired, in the sense that how we construe our experiences of our emotions, is learned in the process of being reared, educated, and enculturated. Initially our experiences of emotions, when they occur, are inchoate and limited to pleasure and pain: our reactions are very simple; we smile or wince, laugh or cry at what we find pleasant or unpleasant. Gradually we discriminate among more and more feelings, associating each with certain circumstances. In this we are conceptualizing what we feel, and inevitably the discriminating and associating occurs in the context of being guided by a parent and later by others. After a time, we respond automatically, as if our conceptualization of what we feel were perfectly natural and inexorable. At that point feelings present themselves in certain ways rather than our construing them in certain ways. And because the guidance we receive is integral to our rearing, and so to our enculturation, at that point we are enculturated in the particular respects.

What is of greatest significance for us about the tailoring and coloring of feelings by enculturation is that as one might well expect, the manner in which individuals are trained to deal with their emotional responses significantly determines how they deal with elective death. This is the case whether the individuals in question are dealing with their own elective-death decisions or the decisions of their spouses, partners, relatives, or friends. It is also the case with respect to those who are counseling others about their own choices to die or the choices to die of those close to them.

To return to an expression introduced in Chapter 1, rather than thinking in terms of learning to conceptualize particular feelings, we can think of individuals' experience-organizing narratives or EONs as shaped by enculturation to better grasp how individuals come to see events around them and within themselves as they do. However, establishing how individuals' perceptions of and reasoning about elective death actually are directly and indirectly conditioned by culturally determined feelings is extraordinarily difficult to do because of lack of knowledge of operant influences and lack of correctness-criteria. The former lack has to do with not knowing just what cultural factors conditioned an individual's feelings. The latter has to do with how even when we are reasonably confident that we have identified one or another iconic or coincidental cultural influence, we have no reliable standards to judge if we are right or wrong about the effects on individuals.

It seems the best we can do is to consider individual cases and see how each looks to us in light of understanding that enculturation does play a major role in every case – an understanding that regrettably is seldom employed or even achieved. This is the vital point: in dealing with elective-death survivors, there needs to be understanding that their feelings are not givens, not natural, unaffected reactions to their spouses', partners', relatives', or friends' choices to die. Survivors' feelings must be recognized as being complexly conditioned, and therefore as possibly misleading or deceptive regarding just what the emotions are that are fueling their responses to electors' choices. This is the heart of everything said in this chapter: however elusive their roles, iconic and coincidental cultures influence survivors' perceptions of and reasoning about electors' choices to die.

To proceed, I offer a hypothetical example, put together from elements of actual cases, to illustrate how iconic and coincidental cultural influences affect survivors and how despite the difficulties acknowledged earlier, particular influences on them can be inferred from their behavior.

George was a man in his late sixties, a staunch Catholic, and a retired engineer. Of special importance regarding George's career was that it had been characterized by resourcefulness and a measure of inventiveness. Over his lifetime and career, George developed and refined an EON that incorporated the main elements of his faith, salient aspects of his work-experience, and his training-honed capacity to often come up with original solutions to the technical problems he faced. George's wife, Edith, was diagnosed with ALS (amyotropic lateral sclerosis, or Lou Gehrig's disease). The progression of ALS is slow, and Edith faced a future of increasing incapacity and a steadily worsening condition. Mindful of the case of Sue Rodriguez, and assured by her physician that while medication could alleviate her symptoms, it could not improve her condition, Edith opted for elective death at a time of her own choosing and while she was still able to end her own life without needing to rely on help from others.[14] George categorically opposed her decision.

On the advice of her physician, Edith and George were receiving some counseling. It became evident during their first couple of counseling sessions that two main factors were operant in George's opposition to Edith's decision. However, these factors did not emerge because George volunteered the information; it was not even clear that aside from his love for Edith and his dread of her dying, he himself was initially aware of just why he opposed Edith's decision as ardently as he did. As is common in these cases, it was when George was pressed and inadvertently angered by the counselor that it became clear how he really felt.

At first George voiced his opposition to his wife's decision in terms of her being precipitous. In this George was taking the most familiar line of argument against elective-death decisions. It was only when the counselor tried to convince George of the hopelessness of Edith's prospects that he angrily revealed the first factor operant in his opposition, blurting out that suicide is sinful. Anger also

---

[14] Mullens, Anne. 1996. *Timely Death: Considering Our Last Rights*, New York: Alfred A. Knopf.

prompted articulation of the second reason for George's opposition to Edith's decisions. In a subsequent counseling session, at one point he again became angry and again blurted out what was really on his mind. On this occasion his complaint was that the negative prognosis and treatment options Edith's physician had given her were short-sighted because they ignored increasingly rapid advances in medical research.

At the risk of oversimplification, I have made the cultural influences on George obvious: his religion and his career. With respect to his religion, George's iconic enculturation inculcated profound agreement with the Catholic doctrine prohibiting elective death; with respect to his career, his coincidental enculturation inculcated an equally profound optimism regarding technological innovation. But simple though this example may be, there were inevitable complications. The complication one would naturally expect was that the iconic and coincidental cultural influences on George were accompanied and reinforced by the effects of influences from his affective states, the main one being his distress over Edith's condition and suffering. Aside from the evident upsetness his emotions caused, what was much less obvious was that much of George's affective resistance to Edith's decision was due to fear-driven psychological avoidance of the imminence of her death. As a consequence of this sublimation, the effects of the iconic and coincidental influences on George were aggravated by being made more compelling than they otherwise might have been. In particular, George fastened on the idea that new or different treatment was or would shortly be available, even if at an experimental stage, and would significantly improve Edith's condition and prospects. Another sublimated affective effect was that George felt at a loss as to how to deal with Edith's discomfort and what he took to be her despair. As a consequence of his feeling of impotence, George was still more adamant about Edith's physician either ignoring or being ignorant of treatment possibilities that might make all the difference to her situation and prospects.

The core of George's response to Edith's elective-death decision had two main components. One component, the affective one, was his dread of Edith's death from ALS, and hence his even greater dread of her earlier elective death. The cultural component was his inability to reconcile her decision with his own religious beliefs and learned attitudes. What primarily concerns us in this chapter is the cultural component. In this example, George's response to Edith's decision is designed to illustrate how his perception of her situation and his assessment of her choice were affected by influences arising from iconic enculturation through his rearing and education and from coincidental enculturation through his training and work experience.

However simple the foregoing example may seem, complications quickly become evident. For instance, while perceptive counselors would have quickly picked up on both George's religious views and his career-based expectations and attitudes, it is less probable that counselors would have as readily discerned the iconic and coincidental cultural influences on their own perceptions and assessments. For example, one possibility is that a counselor in his or her mid-thirties might have been working with questionable but unrealized or at least unacknowledged expectations about the attitudes of a man in his late sixties. Such expectations might have led a younger counselor to take George's negative reaction to Edith's prognosis and decision merely as an age-related inflexibility regarding anything threatening change, and so that counselor might not have delved deeper and achieved a more productive understanding of George's thinking. Similarly, there might have been gender-based expectations prompting a female counselor to see George's opposition to Edith's decision as a typically masculine unwillingness to lose control over his wife's circumstances. Expectations of this sort would have prevented the affected counselors from adequately grasping and appreciating the nature of George's opposition to Edith's decision. Admittedly, misreadings of the kind in question might have been only partly wrong, in being more errors of emphasis than imposition of factors not present in George's opposition, but whether errors of emphasis or actual impositions, the misreadings would have been counterproductive products of iconic or coincidental cultural influences.

With respect to the two main iconic and coincidental cultural influences on George, what was needed was for him to understand how the two main elements of his opposition to Edith's decision, his religious beliefs and confidence in the availability of more efficacious treatments, were more products of his own history than of his and Edith's immediate circumstances. Once George understood the real grounds of his opposition, he would have been able to appreciate that Edith either did not share his religious beliefs or had come to terms with her own religious beliefs, and that his confidence regarding treatments needed to be tempered by better comprehension of the medical reality of Edith's condition and prospects. It may well be that George better understanding the influences on him would not have led him to change his mind about opposing Edith's decision, but the point here is not to change survivors' minds. The point is to insure the soundness of their reasoning by making them aware of iconic and coincidental cultural influences on them.

Gaining awareness of cultural influences is of the utmost importance. This importance is evident in how perhaps the single most consequential cultural influence on elective-death survivors is whether or not certain emotions and the feelings they prompt are acknowledged as of any consequence or even acknowledged. For instance, iconic or coincidental culturally dictated stoicism may not tolerate acknowledgment of some feelings or of the emotions that prompt them, and this can seriously muddle survivors' reasoning. The other side of the coin is cultural imposition of feelings. Enculturation may instill expectations regarding the appropriateness of certain feelings in some situations. If these feelings do not occur, other feelings may be distorted or feelings may be fabricated because of conviction that they should be felt in the circumstances. A typical sort of case that covers both failure to acknowledge and distortion or fabrication of feelings is where what survivors actually feel, when electors who have been suffering greatly choose to die, is relief for themselves and for the electors. Survivors may not be able to admit to feeling relief, having been enculturated to believe that what they should be feeling is great loss and grief. The relief and what underlies it, then, are not acknowledged and as alluded to in a previous chapter, feelings of relief or closure may then be falsely recast as feelings of sorrow and bereavement. Sometimes this recasting will prove innocuous, but sometimes it will produce suppressed guilt and remorse that both distort survivors' thinking in the event and have subsequent damaging psychological consequences.

Efforts to alert survivors to iconic and coincidental cultural influences is significantly thwarted by two serious lacks: our lack of dependable, adequate knowledge of the iconic and coincidental factors most likely influencing survivors, and our lack of correctness criteria for determining when specific cultural factors are influentially operant. These lacks are why what is of foremost importance with respect to dealing with iconic and coincidental cultural influences is dialogue. This is the point made in *Choosing to Die* regarding electors' reasoning and decisions, but it now needs to be made with respect to elective-death survivors' responses to electors' choices to die.

Fortunately for all concerned, the necessary dialogue does not have to be particularly sophisticated nor even broadly informed. What really matters is that dialogue raise as credible a number of points of view on elective death that differ significantly from survivors' own views, and that end can be accomplished without the contributors to dialogue being especially knowledgeable. What is of primary importance is that survivors hear others offer diverse construals of their spouses', partners', relatives', and friends' choices to die, and that they appreciate the implications of the voiced diversity. Survivors need to hear others' views on electors' choices and be open to the import of those views, which is that there are alternatives to their own perceptions and assessments of electors' choices. However, the alternatives cannot be only interpretive variants from within survivors' own iconic and coincidental cultures. The dialogue survivors engage in must be multicultural. This is a key point: participants in the dialogue need to be from different iconic and coincidental cultures if survivors are to identify and reflect on their own cultures' influences on their perceptions and reasoning.

There is, of course, no magic in dialogue. Contrary to what some readers may have thought about my recourse to dialogue in *Choosing to Die*, I neither claimed nor believe that dialogue can itself resolve survivors' problems and dilemmas.[15] To think so would be jejune. What I do believe is that survivors need to participate in multicultural dialogue about electors' choices in order to do two things: first, to achieve awareness of alternatives to their attitudes and construals regarding electors' choices, and second, to use that awareness to better understand the cultural influences on their own thinking and so to gain a more detached perspective on their own attitudes and construals.

---

[15] Young 2008.

CHAPTER SUMMARY

Depending on our ethnicity, place of birth, rearing, and education we are all members of one or another iconic culture. Occasionally people cross over from one to another iconic culture, often because of marriage or emigration to another country. Much less well recognized is that we are also members of coincidental cultures, and often of several coincidental cultures depending on our activities. While there is widespread awareness that iconic cultural values and practices influence our perceptions of situations, our judgments about situations, and what we take into account in our reasoning, there is less awareness that iconic cultural values and practices influence us in so extensive a manner that little we think or do escapes conditioning to one or another degree. What is much less well realized or known is that our perceptions, judgments, and reasoning are equally influenced by values and practices acquired in becoming members of coincidental cultures that characterize where we work, where we live, where we go or went to school, where and with whom we socialize, and even the temporary cooperative projects in which we involve ourselves.

Elective-death survivors concerned to respond as rationally and supportively as they can to their spouses', partners', relatives', and friends' choices to die must reflect seriously and conscientiously on what iconic and coincidental cultural influences may be conditioning their perceptions of and reasoning about electors' choices. In particular, they need to examine closely whether the feelings they have regarding electors' choices are genuine and what emotions actually prompted them because cultural influences almost certainly have conditioned what they feel just as much as their perceptions and reasoning.

The elusive nature of iconic and coincidental cultural influences mean that the most practically effective means for survivors to achieve awareness of cultural influences on their perceptions and reasoning is for them to engage in dialogue with people having different iconic and coincidental cultures. It is against the background of others' voiced construals of electors' situations and choices that survivors can become aware of their own cultures' influences on them.

4

Revising the Criterion for Rational Elective Death

The criteria I developed to establish that elective death – suicide, assisted suicide, and requested euthanasia – can be rational have gone through a number of revisions. The first revision was a result of my realization that the criteria were too detailed and extensive to be of practical use. I learned this from objections raised at conferences, from constructive criticism by colleagues and reviewers, but especially from what I can only describe as impatient dismissal of the criteria by the medical practitioners with whom I discussed them.[1] It became clear that the criteria had to be considerably more practical and brief. What also emerged was that since I first formulated the criteria for the first edition of *The Last Choice: Preemptive Suicide in Advanced Age*, a new element entered into the elective-death issue.[2] This element was not new in the sense of being wholly novel, but in the sense of becoming significant after previously being of minor consequence. The element was the role of multiculturalism in elective-death decisions and their assessment.

Aside from meeting the related needs of brevity and practicality, the considerably revised and amalgamated criterion I presented in *Choosing to Die: Elective Death and Multiculturalism* was not only simpler in its formulation, it was tailored to acknowledge the increasingly weighty role of multiculturalism in the making and assessing of elective-death

---

[1] Prado 2008, iv–v.
[2] Prado 1990.

decisions.[3] As the previous chapter makes clear, multiculturalism has greatly complicated the establishing of the rationality of choosing to die by introducing complexities relating to the influence of iconic cultural values and beliefs on the reasoning and motivation of electors and the perceptions and reasoning of survivors, counselors, health-care professionals, and others assessing electors' decisions. Furthermore, as I argued in *Choosing to Die* and in the previous chapter, recognition and appreciation of the role of iconic culture in elective-death decisions and their assessment quickly leads to recognition and appreciation of coincidental cultural influences and the need to address their impact on agents' and assessors' thinking.

The previous chapter makes apparent that dealing with iconic and coincidental cultural influences on elective-death perceptions and reasoning is too complex a matter to be dealt with in a productive way by relying only on preestablished criteria, no matter how practical the criteria may be. As was pointed out earlier, if the criteria provided in fact are brief and practical enough to be readily applicable, they are more or less useless because they are so general as to be nearly vacuous; by contrast, if they are detailed enough to be pertinent to the making and assessment of elective-death decisions in particular cases, they become hopelessly elaborate as well as too narrowly applicable. This is why I contend that it is necessary that multicultural dialogue complement use of the rationality criterion by electors, survivors, counselors, physicians, and all others needing to sort out iconic and coincidental influences on elective-death decisions and assessment of those decisions.

Despite the necessity of multicultural dialogue, the basic question of whether elective death is rational in particular cases cannot be answered by recourse to dialogue alone. Such recourse is indispensable and will normally prove helpful, but a more fundamental and objective basis is necessary for determining if choosing to die is rational. This is why a criterion for rational elective death is required, one that addresses the question of the logical soundness of electors' reasoning and the acceptability of their motivation.

The consideration of a criterion of rational elective death that follows here is to a great extent determined by the difficulty of dealing

[3] Prado 2008.

with iconic and coincidental cultural influences on a purely criterial basis. Because of that difficulty, the criterion for rational elective death must include – it must require – recourse to the evaluative role of multicultural dialogue. The fact that the criterion cannot be formulated to provide explicit direction for the estimation and evaluation of cultural influences does not lessen, much less does it obviate, the necessity of employing multicultural dialogue in the assessment of the rationality of elective-death reasoning and especially of the acceptability of elective-death motivation. Therefore, in the following revision of the criterion for the use of survivors we must include reference to multicultural evaluative dialogue.

The criteria I introduced in the first edition of *The Last Choice* ended up as a single criterion with two clauses in *Choosing to Die*. This criterion seems to me succinct and clear enough to be practically applicable while still capturing what is essential to rational elective death. However, the criterion is intended and phrased to be applicable to the issue of the rationality of elective death without consideration of who is applying it. That is, as it stands the criterion is applicable to contemplated acts of elective death by electors considering suicide, assisted suicide, or requested euthanasia, as well as by survivors, counselors, physicians, and others concerned to assess the rationality of electors' reasoning, motivation, and decisions. What is needed now is a reformulation of the criterion that facilitates its application by electors' spouses or partners, relatives and friends by incorporating recognition of survivors' relationships with and emotional ties to electors. The reformulation is necessary because the relationships between electors and their spouses or partners, and their close relatives and friends, interlace their respective interests in a way that disallows considering electors' interests to the exclusion of survivors' interests.

In reformulating the criterion, I do not intend to alter its substance, meaning only to formulate it so as to make it amenable to use by survivors. The aim is to enable those closest to electors to understand electors' choices to die while taking into account how electors' choices and their enactment affect them as survivors. As mentioned above, the original criterion is applicable as it stands by electors and anyone else involved with electors' decisions, but survivors pose a special problem because of their personal stakes in electors' circumstances. The danger with further reformulation of the criterion is undoing the succinctness that was gained through earlier revisions. Nonetheless, a little expansion is tolerable and in any case unavoidable. The thing is to keep the expansion to a minimum while making it suffice to serve the special needs of survivors.

As articulated in *Choosing to Die*, the criterion for rational elective death – suicide, assisted suicide, or requested euthanasia – ran as follows:

Criterion A: Autonomous self-killing in terminal illness is rational if choosing to die follows on sound reasoning about pertinent facts, including that death may be annihilation, and cross-cultural deliberative dialogue finds it best serves the agent's interests.[4]

Criterion A consists of two clauses, one clause covering reasoning and the other clause covering motivation. We need to separate the two clauses to proceed. To facilitate reference and avoid misunderstandings, then, the first clause of criterion A is: "Autonomous self-killing in terminal illness is rational if choosing to die follows on sound reasoning about pertinent facts, including that death may be annihilation." The second clause of criterion A is: "and cross-cultural deliberative dialogue finds it best serves the agent's interests."

The first thing to do here is to tweak the wording of the criterion's first clause to make it as brief as possible without altering its substance. The second thing is to temporarily put aside the second clause, that is, reference to agents' interests and cross- or multicultural dialogue, for reasons that will become clear in a moment. I believe the following formulation preserves the criterion's first clause's substance while trimming a few excess words:

Criterion B: Autonomous self-killing in terminal illness is rational if it follows on informed, sound reasoning and acknowledgment that death may be annihilation.

To clarify the content and force of criterion B, or criterion A's slightly reworded first clause, we can briefly review their elements that were argued for at length in formulating criterion A in *Choosing to Die*. These were as follows: (i) elective death must be autonomous to be rational. That is, it cannot be forced in any way. This includes

[4] Prado 2008, 148.

that the option of elective death arising because of electors' dire circumstances and bleak prospects should not of itself be compelling and allowed to override good reasons for not ending one's life or delaying doing so. Given autonomy of choice and action, (ii) elective-death reasoning must be sound in the sense of not containing logical errors, not involving invalidly drawn or unsupported conclusions, and not including false premises. In connection with this latter point, (iii) elective-death reasoning must be free of unproven or unprovable beliefs that are being used as factual premises or facts in premises. In particular, and regardless of widespread beliefs and convictions about an afterlife, to be sound elective-death reasoning must include recognition that ending one's life may well be annihilating oneself.[5] Finally, (iv) elective-death reasoning must be informed reasoning; that is, electors must have the pertinent information regarding their conditions and prognoses and not be under some illusion about their prospects or be mistaken about their conditions – for instance, believing that they are terminally ill when they in fact are not, or believing they have only weeks or days of tolerable life left to them when available treatment offers them considerably more viable time.

It will be clear from the statement of the original criterion A that the criterion's first clause concerns assessment of the soundness of elective-death reasoning while its second clause, in referring to the agent's interests, actually concerns itself with assessment of elective-death motivation. The significance of this in the present context is that aside from its greater succinctness, criterion A differs most markedly from my earlier criteria for rational elective death by requiring culturally diverse viewpoints in assessment of motivation. By temporarily setting aside reference to culturally diverse viewpoints and agents' interests, the slightly rephrased criterion B – the first clause of criterion A – is made applicable only to reasoning about rational elective death. Therefore criterion B is equally applicable by electors to their own reasoning and by survivors and others to electors' reasoning so does not need to be tailored for use by survivors, as long as what they focus on is electors' reasoning. The first clause of criterion A and the whole of criterion B are about reasoning *per se*, hence

---

5 Prado 2008, 26–110. Again, readers interested in the issue are encouraged to read the Appendix.

they are universal or applicant-indifferent in the sense that they may be used by electors, survivors, and anyone else concerned to assess elective-death reasoning.

The second clause of criterion A, referring to interests and multicultural dialogue, does not as it stands lend itself to application equally by electors, survivors, and others because its focus is strictly on electors' motives in the sense of whether those motives best serve electors' interests. The second clause makes no reference to survivors' interests, whether they be their own interests or mutual interests arising from survivors' relationships with electors. What now needs to be done, then, is to supplement criterion B with a second clause to make it applicable to electors' motivation and to be so in a manner that enhances its application by survivors. The complication, as we saw in previous chapters, is the need to work in survivors' emotional involvement with electors as well as their own interests in electors' continuing to live. The major part of the complication is that from electors' perspectives, it normally is not in their best interests to live through more of the natural progressions of their terminal illnesses than they need to, while from survivors' perspectives, electors' continuing to live as long as possible is most commonly in survivors' interests.

But there is more. In criterion A, recourse to cross- or multicultural dialogue had as its point enabling electors to consider alternative understandings of their situations and intentions in order to better and more objectively assess their own motives for ending their lives. In supplementing criterion B with a second clause addressing motivation, we need to do so in such a way that survivors not only can use it to assess electors' reasoning and motivation as acceptable or unacceptable, and do so in light of their own interests in electors' continuing to live as long as possible, but also conduct their assessments sensitive to iconic and coincidental cultural influences on their own perceptions and reasoning.

At this point readers may be wondering how it can be feasible to formulate an elective-death criterion given the requirements just listed. What needs to be clarified in partial answer to this worry is that the aim is not to produce a criterion that will of itself decidedly indicate the soundness of electors' reasoning and motivation, much less provide survivors with resolution of the question of how to deal with electors' choices to die. Application of the criterion is not a matter of simply working through a list of requirements and confirming or disconfirming that they are satisfied. Application of the criterion is a matter of assessing whether electors' reasoning and motivation are sufficiently close to the criterion's requirements that electors' choices can be deemed rational. With respect to application of the criterion by survivors, that is a matter of them not only assessing electors' reasoning and motivation, but also their own responses to electors' decisions by asking themselves probing questions about their perceptions of and reasoning about electors' choices to die: questions that survivors need to ask and answer to gauge the degree to which they are being moved by their own and shared interests, and which those counseling survivors need to insure are asked and answered. Furthermore, as I have argued, the probing questions must also address the matter of how survivors' iconic and coincidental cultures may be coloring their judgments about electors' reasoning and motivation.

As noted earlier, the first clause of criterion A, the criterion presented in *Choosing to Die*, as well as the slightly rephrased version presented earlier, criterion B, are directed on elective-death reasoning and specify that autonomous elective death is rational, as stated in criterion B, "if it follows on informed, sound reasoning and acknowledgment that death may be annihilation." The second clause of criterion A, which was temporarily put aside in the phrasing of criterion B, requires that for elective death to be rational, it not only must satisfy the first clause's requirements, it also must be established through "cross-cultural deliberative dialogue" that elective death "best serves the agent's interests." It is a version of this second clause that we need to add to criterion B, which at this point makes no reference to interests and hence to motivation. To continue, we need to clarify how motivation and interests are connected in the phrasing of the second clause of criterion A.

The pivotal point here is that motives either do or do not serve agents' best interests. If they do not, it is because the motives are misguided or misconceived; that is, they are based on false information, misunderstandings, erroneous beliefs, or interpretive mistakes – allowing, of course, for motives with psychopathological roots that do not concern us here. Of course, agents may be motivated to act in ways contrary to their own interests for the sake of another or others, or for a cause or ideal, but in such cases agents are aware that their motives do not serve their own interests except, perhaps, in some extended sense involving fittingness or satisfaction. It is the fact that motives do or do not serve agents' interests that requires that the phrasing of criterion A's second clause be in terms of interests rather than specifically in terms of motives. The second clause is concerned with the acceptability of motivation, paralleling the first clause's concern with the acceptability of reasoning, but the fact that some motives may not serve agents' best interests means that phrasing the second clause expressly in terms of motives runs a significant risk. The risk is that electors' motives may be assessed for acceptability solely on their inherent value, rather than being assessed for acceptability with respect to how they do or do not serve electors' interests.

The foregoing point relates directly to the necessity of multicultural dialogue in assessment of electors' motivation because from the perspective of iconic or coincidental cultural values, electors' motives may appear acceptable and even admirable despite their being contrary to electors' best interests. Assessment of the acceptability of electors' motives for choosing to die requires that their motives be weighed both with respect to how they affect electors' interests and with respect to their inherent value. The inclusion of reference to cross-cultural dialogue in criterion A's second clause addressed the concern that electors might be choosing to die because of iconic and coincidental cultural factors influencing them in questionable or at least arguable ways. The aim of the clause was that culturally diverse input in dialogue alert electors to alternative views of their situations and choices and thereby enable them to reflect more objectively on their own cultural values and practices and hence on the influences those values and practices might be exerting on them. The supplementation of criterion B with a second clause, then, must incorporate multicultural assessment of whether electors' motives serve their best interests, and as should now be clear, phrasing of the supplementary clause must be in line with criterion A's second clause and be in terms of interests rather than motives.

The supplementation of criterion B is about producing a second clause that not only relates to effective assessment of electors' motivation, but makes the resulting criterion applicable to electors' reasoning and motivation by spouses, partners, relatives, and friends in a manner that recognizes how survivors' perceptions and assessments of electors' choices to die are inescapably tied to and influenced by both their emotions and feelings and by how survivors construe shared and their own interests in relation to electors' deaths. As we have considered, it is both virtually impossible and in fact wrong-headed to try to separate survivors' responses to electors' choices to die from the affective factors that unquestionably condition those responses. It is crucially important, therefore, that survivors identify and reflect on the influences exerted on their perceptions and reasoning by their affective states and by their iconic and coincidental cultures, and reference to survivors' interests in the second clause is the briefest and perhaps the most effective way to prompt them to engage in the called-for reflection.

Packing all of this into a clause to supplement criterion B looks to be a daunting task. However, the task looks a little less daunting when we consider a significant point about the purpose of the criterion we are trying to frame. The criterion's purpose is not to set or change survivors' thinking regarding electors' choices. The criterion cannot be a rule determining survivors' responses to electors' decisions. No preestablished criterion could possibly serve that end without being hopelessly rigid and doctrinaire. The proposed criterion's purpose is to insure that survivors' thinking is sound and that their affective inclinations are properly examined. The criterion is intended to be an assessment standard, not a resolution device. The point of producing a criterion for assessment of elective death for use by individuals including those having intimate or very close relationships with those choosing to die is to insure that elective-death survivors properly assess electors' choices by identifying, understanding, and to a proper extent accommodating or restraining the role their emotions and feelings play in how they weigh and assess their spouses', partners', relatives', and friends' elective-death reasoning and motivation.

Criterion B states the requirements for assessing the reasoning aspect of electors' choices, and as we have noted, its employment is neutral with respect to who applies it. It is worth reiterating that in essence, the requirements are that for their elective deaths to be rational, electors must freely and knowingly choose to end their lives and do so, or in some cases – and in the appropriate moral and legal circumstances – request others to end their lives for them due to their inability to do so themselves. Additionally, the bases for their free choices must include adequate knowledge of their actual conditions and prospects and their reasoning must be sound in the logical sense that they must reach conclusions that follow validly from true premises. This latter condition rules out electors relying on unproven beliefs, which means that elective-death reasoning must proceed on the basis that ending one's life may result in cessation of existence of the self in any mode or form. The extent to which these requirements can be fully met is, of course, an unknown and unestablishable matter, given human nature, but the point is that every effort must be made to meet the requirements. If this is done, then the choice to die can be deemed a rational decision and consequent act.

The central reason why criterion A complemented its first or reasoning clause with a clause about multicultural assessment of motivation was that it could happen that some electors choosing to die might satisfy the requirements for acting autonomously, reasoning soundly, and being cognizant of likely consequences, but fall short of being rational regarding their motives for choosing to die because, though their motives might be rational in themselves, they do not serve electors' interests. This is the point of our concern that if the criterion's second clause is stated in terms of motives rather than in terms of interests, electors' motives could misguidedly be taken at face value and not be assessed with respect to whether they serve electors' interests.

The most common motive for elective death in terminal illness is those afflicted wanting to avoid enduring further pointless suffering for the sake of a little more time – a few weeks or even months that will be filled either with only more of the same discomforts and despair as the previous weeks and months or with even less desirable alternations between pain and medicated wooziness or drugged sleep. Of course, there usually are other motives, some of which may be rational, such as not wanting to further burden loved ones, while some may be less than rational, such as wanting and expecting to be reunited with a deceased spouse in the afterlife.

Assuming that electors' motives are acceptable on a purely rational basis, what needs to be determined is whether those motives also best serve electors' interests. However, assessment of electors' motivation cannot be limited to whether they are choosing to die for rationally acceptable motives that serve their own interests. Consideration needs to be given to whether electors' motives are too uncompromisingly self-centered. For instance, we can imagine individuals who are terminally ill choosing to die after soundly reasoning through their options but without adequately taking into account how further tolerating their conditions for a short time would be greatly valued by those closest to them. It might be that electors tolerating even great discomfort for a week or two longer would enable them to be alive for, say, the birth of a grandchild, which could be of great importance to a son or daughter. This sort of consideration might not weigh heavily enough on electors' minds, given their circumstances, so their choices to die might be rational in a strict sense but not be reasonable in a broader sense because of the difference their continuing to live for a short time would make to survivors. In short, electors' choices to die may be narrowly rational but their motivation be unreasonable, not because of the nature of the motives themselves or whether they serve electors' interests, but because of the integral nature of electors' relationships with survivors and the consequent interconnectedness of their interests with survivors' interests.

The difference there can be between something being rational yet being unreasonable is one that many accept only in an intuitive way and it is important to be clear about this difference regarding the foregoing point. An elector's decision may be rational in that it satisfies the requirements listed above: it follows on sound reasoning and on acceptable, interest-serving motivation. However, that decision may nonetheless be unreasonable in that while it serves the elector's interests, it may disproportionately injure a spouse or partner, relative or friend. We often have to make compromises between doing what best serves our own interests and the interests of others, and this despite our having every right to act in our own best interests. Because of our humanity, this need for compromise remains true even in the case of choosing to serve our interests by ending our lives.

In the case of electors choosing to die, what normally is most centrally at issue regarding their interests is simply time: time during which they must bear precisely what they choose to avoid by electing to die. It may be, however, that a little more sufferance of their situations results in electors honoring their emotional commitments to survivors and enhancing the lives of survivors in significant ways. Despite electors' toleration of their situations longer than they want being to their own detriment, it may be less so than their dying sooner would be to the detriment of the survivors concerned, given the presence and importance of shared interests in close relationships. This is just the sort of consideration that makes the issue of the rationality of elective death so much more difficult when we factor in survivors, their relationships to electors, and hence their interests.

We need now to turn to the formulation of a clause to supplement criterion B in order to produce a criterion that parallels criterion A but one that includes recognition of survivors' interests. As we proceed, it must be kept in mind that the purpose of the criterion is to enable electors, survivors, and concerned others to understand electors' decisions and to assess those decisions as objectively as possible in two respects: the soundness of the reasoning and the acceptability of the motivation.

What we have so far in criterion B is that "autonomous self-killing in terminal illness is rational if it follows on informed, sound reasoning and acknowledgment that death may be annihilation." As has been clarified, this clause deals with how electors reason their way to their decisions to end their lives. The only motivational element implicit in criterion B is the given that electors are moved to reason about ending their lives because they are terminally ill and want to avoid what normal progression of their illnesses has in store for them. This motivational element is a given in the sense that electors would not have cause to reason about ending their lives if they were not terminally ill. Recall that in the present context we are not concerned with individuals who consider ending their lives due to other causes. What is needed, then, is a version of criterion A's second clause, which requires that for elective death in terminal illness to be rational, not only must the reasoning be sound, but "cross-cultural deliberative dialogue" must find that elective death "best serves the agent's interests."

It should be clear that reference to cross-cultural or multicultural dialogue is not limited to iconic cultures; the reference includes coincidental cultures. This point is evident in the example of George and Edith. We saw that George's opposition to Edith's elective death is based on his belief that it is wrong to take one's own life and his belief that Edith is disastrously underestimating what medical science has to offer her. Of course, George also does not want to see Edith die because of his love for her and the centrality in both their lives of their relationship of many years, but this more general aspect of George's opposition to Edith's decision is a given and open to assessment only in terms of whether his affection and dread are impeding or distorting his understanding of Edith's decision. What is important here is that, in sum, George's more specific opposition to Edith's elective-death decision was reduced to two operant beliefs directly opposed to Edith's basic premises. George believed self-killing wrong, whereas Edith believed that it is permissible to end one's own life in some circumstances; George believed that medical science had more to offer Edith, whereas she believed her physician was right that she had exhausted her treatment options.[6]

To better understand the conflict between George and Edith, and the interplay of iconic and coincidental cultural influences, consider again the case of the king's horseman. We can readily imagine disagreeing with the horseman's premise that he must end his life to continue serving his king in an afterlife because of not believing in survival after death or at least not the sort of survival the horseman envisions.[7] Why I mention the case of the king's horseman here is to highlight that to most members of a Western iconic culture, the case of the king's horseman looks to be just the sort of case calling for multicultural dialogue to bring out different perspectives and thereby prompt the horseman to reexamine his beliefs and decision. But to these same individuals, the case of George and Edith would not appear to call for multicultural dialogue. This is too insular a view, and it is so because it focuses exclusively on iconic cultural differences.

George and Edith certainly shared a broadly defined iconic culture: both were members of the Western Christian iconic culture. However, George and Edith were also members of disparate, more narrowly defined iconic cultures. George's more specific iconic cultural background was Catholic, and his enculturation prohibited

[6] Hartocollis, Anemona, 2009, "At the End, Offering Not a Cure but Comfort," *New York Times*, Aug. 20, 2009, 1, 16–17.

[7] Soyinka 2002.

elective death. Edith's more specific iconic culture was Protestant in denomination. Additionally, she majored in philosophy in university and left organized religion in her senior year. These factors provided a background that enabled her to believe in the permissibility of elective death in certain circumstances. In addition, George and Edith were members of disparate coincidental cultures. George had a long and continuous career as an engineer, while Edith held a number of different positions during her working life and so was exposed to various work-related coincidental cultures. George's career-based coincidental culture was what instilled in him his confidence in scientific and technological innovation. This was an influence absent in Edith's case. It is because of such disparities between electors' and survivors' coincidental cultures, disparities that may be as significant as those between iconic cultures, that multicultural dialogue is necessary in assessment of all cases of elective death.

To continue, then, criterion A's second clause calls for multicultural assessment of elective-death decisions regarding whether choosing to die best serves electors' interests. Supplementation of criterion B with a new second clause must begin with the same requirement because the fundamental question that must be addressed after application of the reasoning clause is whether elective-death motivation is acceptable, and as we have seen, that is essentially a matter of determining whether elective death best serves electors' interests. However, because the new criterion is to be applied by spouses and partners, relatives and friends, as well as by concerned others, the target now must be not only determining whether elective death best serves electors' interests, but also how it affects survivors' interests. However, because it is inevitable that electors' deaths will harm survivors' interests to some extent, the question is whether electors' deaths harm survivors to a great enough extent as to render electors' motivation unacceptable. Assessing the extent to which elective death harms survivors is, of course, a matter of looking at individual cases. What is necessary at the criterial level is the inclusion of survivors' interests in the rationality criterion's requirements.

The most straightforward way to factor in survivors' interests into the elective-death criterion is to introduce reference to their interests in its second clause. But doing so is a little delicate. We could, for

instance, formulate the second clause as elective death being rational if "multicultural assessment determines it best serves both the
agent's and survivors' interests." However, this formulation and others similar to it give survivors' interests too important a place in the
assessment of electors' motivation. What is being assessed is, after all,
whether electors' motives for taking their own lives are acceptable in
that they best serve electors' interests. Survivors' interests need to be
referred to, but they cannot be put on the same footing as electors'
interests. Reference to survivors' interests, then, must be more qualified than the foregoing phrase and others like it.

Before suggesting a better formulation of the called-for second
clause, I need to clarify that while the intent is to produce an elective-
death criterion that is applicable by electors' spouses, partners, relatives, and friends to electors' reasoning and motivation, the revised
criterion cannot be so phrased that it is applicable only by survivors.
Criterion B and the first clause of criterion A are applicant-neutral
since they have to do with the soundness of elective-death reasoning. The called-for second clause addressing motivation criterion B
cannot be applicant-specific. To make it so would be to produce one
criterion for survivors and another for everyone else, including electors themselves. Doing this would introduce discrepancies in assessments of elective death, and they would be discrepancies due not to
the nature of electors' reasoning and motivation, but merely to who
is doing the assessing. This is unacceptable and would in turn make
the two criterions unworkable. Reference to survivors' interests needs
to be phrased in such a way as to make a single criterion equally
applicable by electors, by those counseling or treating electors, and
by survivors. The trick is to produce a criterion that though not applicant-specific, nonetheless will serve survivors' special needs.

The following is a first approximation of a revised criterion B that
incorporates a possible second clause:

Criterion C: Autonomous self-killing in terminal illness is rational if it follows
on informed, sound reasoning and acknowledgment that death may be
annihilation, and multicultural assessment determines it best serves the
agent's interests without disproportionately harming survivors' interests.

Two points that we need to remember here are that, first, in the
final analysis elective death is the most personal and individualistic

choice a person can make and others' interests, regardless of how close those others may be to electors, must take second place to the interests of those choosing to die. Second, as we saw above, the basic question regarding elective death and survivors' interests is about time: how long electors are willing to wait in order to harm their spouses', partners', relatives', and friends' interests as little as they can. Taken together, these two points indicate that given electors' terminal conditions, the second clause addressing motivation essentially is about the timing of elective death. In other words, given that electors will eventually die of their illnesses, what most directly affects their survivors' interests is how long electors bear their conditions before enacting their choices to die.

In light of the foregoing point about timing, the proposed second clause, "and multicultural assessment determines it best serves the agent's interests without disproportionately harming survivors' interests," is too vague. A better formulation is as follows: "and multicultural assessment determines it best serves agent's interests and is timed to least damage survivors' interests." This latter second clause yields the following criterion:

Criterion D: Autonomous self-killing in terminal illness is rational if it follows on informed, sound reasoning and acknowledgment that death may be annihilation, and multicultural assessment determines it best serves the agent's interests and is timed to least damage survivors' interests.

This formulation is better, but the wording can be revised to make the criterion more intuitive and clearer by lightening its rather technical phrasing. I propose, then, that we proceed on the basis of the following articulation:

Criterion E: Self-killing is rational if autonomous, soundly reasoned, adequately informed, includes acknowledgment death may be personal annihilation, and multicultural assessment determines it best serves one's interests while timed to least harm survivors.

This formulation is more straightforward and shorter than criterion A and D and has the advantage of making more evident the individual requirements for elective death to be rational:

   (i) autonomous choice,
   (ii) sound reasoning,

(iii) adequate information,

(iv) acknowledgment that dying may be annihilation,

(v) multicultural assessment of interests/motivation, and

(vi) recognition of survivors' interests.

Note that I have deleted reference to terminal illness in criterion E. The reason is a welcome development in that as it stands, criterion E is applicable to other cases of elective death where the choice to die is prompted by different causes. For example, criterion E is applicable to preemptive suicide: cases where individuals choose to end their lives in anticipation of conditions they are unwilling to bear even in their earliest stages, such as Alzheimer's or ALS.[8] Note that in the remainder of this chapter and what follows it I will refer to criterion E simply as the criterion for rational elective death or simply "the criterion."

Assuming acceptability of the criterion – and I refer readers to *Choosing to Die* where the various requirements except for (vi) are argued for in detail – we now must address the matter of how the criterion is of special use to survivors.[9]

As considered earlier, electors ending their lives prior to when they would normally die from terminal conditions inevitably harm their survivors' interests. They do so by depriving survivors of themselves as spouses, partners, relatives, and friends. In some cases the deprivation will be measured only in weeks or even days, but given contemporary diagnostic techniques and treatments, in many if not most cases the deprivation will be a matter of months and often even of years, depending on the precise illness and the efficacy of treatment. There are, then, two pairs of considerations to be balanced in assessing whether electors' deaths are timed to least harm survivors.

The first pair of considerations concerns electors and is, on the one hand, electors' desires to end their suffering and, on the other hand, their preparedness to bear their situations longer than they need to for the sake of survivors. The second set of considerations needing to be balanced concerns survivors and is, on the one hand, survivors' desires to have electors live as long as possible and, on the

[8] Prado 1990, 1998.
[9] Prado 2008.

other, their recognition of the benefit to electors of ending their suffering as soon as they can.

How, then, does application of the criterion for rational elective death work in enabling electors and survivors to achieve a proper balance of these temporal considerations? The first thing to note is that application of the criterion immediately raises the question of balance because of the wording of the second clause. That is, the criterion expressly refers to the timing of electors' deaths as it relates to survivors' interests, and this reference disallows electors and survivors ignoring or overlooking the central factor in the interweaving of their respective interests. As it should, then, the criterion raises the question of the balance between elective death serving the interests of electors in a manner that does the least damage to survivors' interests.

In applying the criterion, electors, survivors, attending physicians, counselors, and anyone else concerned with electors' choices to die would proceed in the same way regarding the criterion's first clause. Electors' reasoning about ending their lives needs to be assessed in terms of the first four of the criterion's requirements. That is, electors' reasoning needs to be assessed for the autonomy of their choices to die; for the soundness of their reasoning in the sense of the truth of their premises and the validity of their conclusions; for the adequacy of their information about their conditions and prospects; and for understanding that in ending their lives they may be annihilating themselves as persons. It is with respect to the second clause or the fifth and sixth of the criterion's requirements that survivors diverge from electors and from involved professionals with respect to how the criterion is applied. The divergence centers on the inescapable fact that in assessing elective-death decisions, whether survivors' interests are served or harmed is part of what is at issue.

Our concern here is mainly with survivors, therefore I will consider electors' thinking about their interests and the timing of their elective deaths only briefly. The basic question electors need to ask and answer is how willing – and perhaps psychologically able – they are to bear their conditions a little longer for the sake of their spouses, partners, relatives, and friends. The issue, then, is how much punishing time electors are willing to trade for the good of their spouses, partners, relatives, and friends.

I think that the way electors should approach their deliberations about timing requires their achieving a high level of objectivity with respect to just how important their continuing to live is to survivors. This is a matter of looking hard both at immediate and longer-term effects on survivors. Simply put, it is a matter of trying to determine just how much difference it actually will make to survivors in the present and in the future if electors postpone their deaths and bear their conditions longer. For instance, electors no doubt will value being remembered by a spouse or partner, a relative or friend, as having been willing to endure their conditions longer for the sake of mutual affection and commitment. But electors also must realize and appreciate two things: first, that the central consideration in their circumstances is their interest in ending their suffering, and second, that beyond the immediate present their continued survival for a short period may be as good as for a longer period, if what is in question is the difference their survival will make to survivors.

Electors must also think hard about what they risk by postponing their elective deaths. The major considerations are their waning physical ability to end their own lives and the possible weakening of their resolve and of their psychological ability to end their own lives. In the former case, electors grow increasingly reliant on the help of others, which legal and other considerations may inhibit or obstruct; in the latter case they risk not only losing their determination regarding ending their lives, they also risk their reasoning and/ or motivation being undermined by changes in their situations or in their thinking.

There is another element that many survivors will likely not want to face or to consider in a direct way, and that is the fact that electors' conditions in themselves, and their consequent elective-death decisions, irrevocably alter electors' relationships with survivors. As alluded to earlier, choosing to die to escape an anguished and hopeless existence is, after all, effectively to choose to end all relationships as well as one's life. Under one description, choosing to die, as a decision, is a prioritizing of release and closure over continuing to live in misery and desolation, and prioritizing release and closure entails terminating relationships, no matter how highly valued those relationships may be. Once the choice to die is made, then, relationships are in effect relinquished, however reluctantly, and thus the precedence of the interests of even those survivors closest to electors is abandoned or greatly reduced.

With respect to survivors, application of the criterion should establish the rationality of electors' reasoning and the acceptability of their motivation, but it should also make explicit what many may be reluctant to admit, which is that survivors' interests are decidedly negatively affected by electors' decisions and enactment of those decisions. The criterion's wording, then, is designed to immediately raise the issue of survivors' interests; an issue that might otherwise go unacknowledged. In the process of assessing whether electors' motives best serve their interests, therefore, survivors face questions about how electors' choices affect their own interests. In this way the criterion is not only an evaluative tool, it is an effective prompt for survivors to consider that to be acceptable, electors' motives must take account of interests beyond their own.

This latter point is central and bears repetition. What the criterion does is that along with providing the requirements for the rationality of elective death, it factors into the assessment of electors' motives consideration that their motives not only have to best serve electors' interests, but that they must do so in a way qualified by the interests of their spouses, partners, relatives, and friends. The criterion's second clause is in part a reminder that the interests of individuals in intimate or close relationships cannot be considered in isolation; it is a reminder that the interests of those in intimate or close relationships with others are – to a point – shared with those others.

We come now to a matter mentioned several times before but that needs to considered more carefully. The matter is that survivors need to reflect on affective and cultural influences on their perceptions of and reasoning about electors' decisions. Once the commonality of electors' and survivors' interests is on the table, as it were; once the criterion raises the issue of the qualification of electors' interests by consideration of survivors' interests, then survivors' application of the criterion not only becomes partly an assessment of their own interests in electors' continued life, it also involves reflection on their assessments of electors' reasoning and motivation and how those assessments may be colored or distorted by their own feelings and iconic and coincidental cultures.

This feature, then, is what makes the revised criterion special regarding survivors: survivors cannot properly apply the revised criterion to electors' reasoning and motivation without considering their own interests because the criterion specifically connects electors' and survivors' interests. And in considering their own interests, survivors are in effect forced to consider their thinking about their spouses', partners', relatives', or friends' choices to die. The key to this transition is that survivors cannot properly and adequately examine how their interests are affected by electors' choices without reflection on how they perceive and assess electors' decisions because clearly how they perceive and assess those decisions at least in part determines how they construe the threat to their own and shared interests. For instance, if survivors judge electors to be acting unreasonably or hastily, they will see their own interests as unduly devalued or disregarded. Against this, if survivors judge electors to be acting rationally and best serving their own interests in a timely manner, they will see their own interests as served to the extent that they are least damaged by electors' decisions and acts – just as the criterion requires.

Consider again the case of George and Edith. Instead of imagining that George was told about the criterion for elective death and applied it to Edith's decision, take it that two factors had effectively the same consequences as his using the criterion: first, the counselor had some success in getting George to be more reflective about his opposition to Edith's elective death. Second, Edith's pain increased rather suddenly. As it happened, the physician who attended her because of this new development was not her regular physician, who was unavailable at the time, and George was daunted by the new physician's agreement with Edith's regular physician that her condition was hopeless with respect to treatment that would improve it in any way.

The new physician also told George that there was nothing on the research horizon that suggested, much less promised, significant improvements in treatment. As a result of this fresh perspective on the treatment issue, George was prompted to think again about his coincidental-culture-based conviction that better treatments for Edith either were available or would soon be available. Again, witnessing her increased suffering forced George to reflect on his iconic-culture-instilled prohibition of elective death. This was especially so because of the nearly comatose condition that Edith went into after being given enough medication to relieve her pain. George's newly reflective thinking about Edith's choice to die went something like this:

I want Edith to live as long as possible but I'm beginning to wonder if maybe it's best that she doesn't. Why would God want Edith to suffer as she is suffering? She doesn't deserve it, and it doesn't do any good. Is there such a big difference between Edith refusing treatment and treatment being ineffective or not available? Maybe I'm being too rigid about the suicide part. I'm also no longer so sure that there are better treatments out there or that there will be in time to do her any good. I don't know enough about medicine to know for sure, but the doctors say it's hopeless. Am I letting my beliefs and my need and love for her blind me to how she really would be better off not surviving any longer? She's thought things through very carefully, and she doesn't deserve to suffer to no good end. Am I being too selfish? She's certainly proven to me that she doesn't want to hurt me by ending her life. I think now that she's survived with this pain and hopelessness long enough. If I were in her shoes I'd want it all to end, and it seems time that it does end.

George's second thoughts might have been all to the good, but from one perspective they came too late. Had he been more understanding and less rigid in his own thinking, Edith might have ended her life well before having to face the greater pain she had to endure and the despair accompanying the promise of more of the same or worse. However, what most concerns us here is that despite his initial opposition, George came to understand Edith's decision and, if not to endorse it, at least to accept it. This is the aim of survivors applying the rationality criterion: to understand electors' decisions as well as they can by reflecting on what may be impeding their understanding. Understanding likely will lead to acceptance, but if it does not, at least the nonacceptance by survivors of electors' decisions is an informed and thoughtful one rather than the product of unrecognized affective and cultural influences.

CHAPTER SUMMARY

Establishing that elective death is a rational choice and action requires determining that it is freely chosen and done, that the decision to do it is soundly reasoned on the basis of adequate information and appreciation of consequences, and that its motivation best serves agents' interests. However, few individuals can decide to end their lives, no matter how rationally, without affecting the lives of others. This is especially so when the individuals choosing to die share close relationships with others who will survive them. The interests of the spouses, partners, relatives, and friends of those who choose to die inevitably are harmed by elective death, so although their interests cannot be given priority over those of electors, the need is that their interests are harmed as little as possible. The criterion for rational elective death, then, must include in its requirements that survivors' interests be considered. The question is how best to do this, and the answer seems to be to work the timing of elective death into the requirements.

The diminishment of harm to the interests of survivors can be most effectively achieved by electors timing their deaths just late enough to demonstrate their caring for survivors by maintaining their relationship a little longer than they otherwise might. The price paid by electors for such delays is sufferance of the conditions they seek to escape by choosing to die, but it is the very sufferance of those conditions for a little longer that constitutes their honoring their relationships with survivors. For their part, survivors must recognize that honoring of their relationships and see it as proper consideration of their own interests. Survivors also must use their recognition of electors' honoring of their relationships as cause to be more accepting of earlier elective death.

The conclusion here is that the criterion for rational elective death needs to include requirements dealing with electors' reasoning and motivation as well as reference to survivors' interests. Reference to survivors' interests is best done by specifying that the timing of elective death has to be such that it does the least damage to survivors' interests. In this way, the criterion becomes applicable in a special manner by survivors, while being applicable by anyone else concerned with electors' choices to die. The criterion achieves specialness in application by survivors because in referring to their interests, it in effect forces survivors to reflect on their perceptions of and reasoning about electors' choices to die, and so on affective and cultural influences on their perceptions and reasoning. How this works is that in the process of reflecting on their interests, survivors – because they care for electors – will examine what they see as in their interest and hence will need to consider how their feelings are affecting their perceptions and reasoning. In addition, given the criterion's requirement of multicultural dialogue, they will be prompted to consider iconic and coincidental cultural influences as well.

5

Two Philosophical Challenges

In previous chapters I have apologized for introducing abstract material that might seem out of place in a book concerned mainly with what is, in the end, a very practical matter. As I have explained, the abstract material is necessary to establish a number of points regarding the rationality criterion and its application. In this chapter I consider two philosophical challenges to the rationality criterion and its application. Because of the conceptual nature of both challenges, neither can be dealt with or even be properly presented without recourse to philosophical abstraction; therefore, I will not apologize again for once more delving into the abstract. What I can do is recommend to readers that they consider the two challenges as outlined in the next couple of paragraphs and decide whether they want to read consideration of both. Those who do not feel the first challenge merits detailed consideration can skip to the discussion of the second. As will be clear, though, the second challenge is of real consequence and its discussion needs to be read by everyone before proceeding to Chapter 6.

The two philosophical challenges to the rationality criterion focus on the assessment of elective-death reasoning, though the second spills over into assessment of elective-death motivation. The first challenge is implicit in postmodern critiques of traditional conception of reason and rationality as ahistorical and universal: conception of reason and rationality as not determined by our temporally variable values, beliefs, and practices. The second challenge is an explicit one having to do with beliefs about whether or not death is personal annihilation, and is stated in Margaret Battin's perceptive review of *Choosing to Die*. Battin posed the second challenge in this way:

Prado argues that the rationality criterion requires acknowledgment that death may be annihilation. Here, I think, he sees the issue from only one perspective. He ought also to consider the convinced, secular skeptic's concerns about religions' claims for the possibility of an afterlife, and whether this person's choices about suicide can be rational if he or she fails to acknowledge that death may *not* be annihilation.[1]

I have to admit that this point did not occur to me either in writing *Choosing to Die* or in preparing a good deal of the present book.[2] It was only when I read Battin's review of *Choosing to Die* in September 2009 that I realized she was quite right and that I had dealt with the matter of personal annihilation in too quick and narrow a way. I am grateful to Battin for making this point and try to rectify this lapse later. Before doing so, however, I will discuss the postmodern challenge. This is because as will emerge, the two challenges are perhaps surprisingly interrelated.

In the foregoing chapters I have tried to deal with the variety of perspectival differences regarding elective-death motivation and its assessment by including in the rationality criterion a clause that requires dialogic multicultural treatment of motivation. The point of multicultural dialogue is to introduce different perspectives into the assessment of electors' motives for choosing to die conducted both by electors and by concerned others. The underlying assumption operant in having recourse to multicultural dialogue is that while various culture-determined perspectives on elective death all have legitimacy in their respective cultural contexts, they need to be contrasted and compared with perspectives from outside those contexts to insure that electors' interests are not unduly depreciated by culturally insular assessments. It is the exposure of electors and other assessors to diverse perspectives on electors' motivation, exposure to perspectives

---

[1] Battin, Margaret P., 2009, Review of *Choosing to Die: Elective Death and Multiculturalism*, *Notre Dame Philosophical Reviews*, Sept. 2009, *http://ndpr.nd.edu/reviews.cfm* (search archives for "Prado").

[2] Prado 2008; see also the Appendix.

that differ from their own and which are legitimate in their own cultural contexts, that should enable electors and assessors to better reflect on the iconic and coincidental cultural influences that may be shaping their perceptions and decisions. It is through such exposure that both electors and assessors may be alerted to culturally influenced motives that are contrary to electors' interests.

Throughout the previous chapters I have in effect contrasted perspectivally diverse understanding and assessment of motivation with universalist assessment of reasoning soundness. That is, whereas I have insisted on the importance of examining differing perspectives with respect to assessing elective-death motivation, I have proceeded on the basis that determining the soundness of elective-death reasoning relies on the same principles for everyone, regardless of perspectival differences. No doubt some readers have taken this way of proceeding as manifesting blithe indifference to perspectival diversity regarding reasoning. Contrary to this possible impression, it is not a matter of indifference. What I have been doing is denying, albeit in an implicit manner, the relevance or applicability of perspectival diversity to assessment of reasoning. I have throughout proceeded on the presupposition that assessment of reasoning must be conducted on the basis of universal principles.

It is my view that assessment of elective-death motivation requires perspectival diversity precisely because motives themselves, as well as their assessment, are too conditioned by iconic and coincidental cultural influences to be considered from only one point of view. Perspectival diversity is necessary to enable some distancing and objectivity in the process of first understanding and then assessing elective-death motivation, whether the assessment is conducted by electors themselves or by concerned others. But reason and rationality are not products of culture, despite the fact that their actual application may well be colored by cultural influences. Assessment of elective-death reasoning, while it needs to be sensitive to cultural influences, must be conducted by employing principles that apply equally to everyone and are not products of group, much less individual, perspectives, and that do not differ in their proper application depending on who applies them. For instance, we cannot qualify the deductive-reasoning principle that if one accepts premises as true, one must accept the valid conclusions they lead to or be guilty of self-contradiction. This is not a principle that applies to reasoning in some cultural contexts but not in others.

Unfortunately, because of postmodern critiques of traditional conception of reason and rationality, the universality of rationality, reason, and reasoning principles is no longer accepted as a given. There are many who would maintain that assessing elective-death reasoning requires the same perspectival diversity as does assessing elective-death motivation. I did not acknowledge this point earlier because to have done so would have required me to present what follows at a much earlier stage, and that would have impaired my efforts to set out as clearly as possible the points I have made about the rationality criterion and its application. Had I begun with what I offer in this chapter on reason and rationality's universality and challenges to it, my discussions of feelings and cultures, and my revision of the rationality criterion, would have been inopportunely complicated by the issues inevitably raised by the material that follows.

Those readers who share my acceptance of reason and rationality as universal, as the same for everyone, need not work through discussion of this first challenge to the rationality criterion. The trouble, however, is that the issue of perspectival differences on rationality and reason cannot be ignored. Intellectual integrity demands that the matter be considered if there has been significant appeal to reasoning and rationality, and there certainly has been such appeal in previous chapters. The universality of reason and rationality can no longer be assumed, hence it is necessary to consider the matter here in order not to leave the rationality criterion vulnerable to charges that it naively presupposes something that is currently the topic of extensive debate.

To proceed, I draw on another area in philosophy that has very much interested me: Foucault's postmodernism and critique of traditional philosophy. As my remarks in Chapter 2 indicate, I have done a fair bit of work on Foucault, and consider that his views represent the most serious and viable postmodern challenge to established conceptions of reason and rationality.[3]

---

[3] Prado, C. G., 1995, *Starting with Foucault: An Introduction to Genealogy*, Boulder, CO, and New York: Westview Press; 2000c; 2003; 2005; 2006; 2009a, *Foucault's Legacy*, ed. London: Continuum Books.

THE FIRST CHALLENGE

The basic problem we face regarding the implicit challenge that assessment of elective-death reasoning must be perspectival is that postmoderns reject what I have assumed in previous chapters, namely, that reasoning must be assessed on the basis of universal principles, such as that of logical validity. For postmoderns, assessment of elective-death reasoning must be done on the basis of a diversity of viewpoints, including both cultural and individual ones. We encountered a naive version of postmodernist relativism in Chapter 1, when I considered what I there called "cognitive libertarianism."[4] However, the relativism that defines postmodernism is considerably more sophisticated than that of cognitive libertarianism and has a philosophical basis that goes back to Friedrich Nietzsche and eventually to Protagoras.

The basic claim postmodernists make in rejecting the universality of rationality and reason is perhaps best and certainly most briefly articulated in Foucault's contention that "reason is self-created."[5] What he meant by saying reason is self-created is that reason and rationality are historical; that is, they are products of temporally and regionally different intellectual values, different past and present ideologies, and contextually different justificatory practices, all of which jointly determine how reason and rationality are conceived and how they are used in different historical periods and social and learned milieus.

It was Foucault's conception of reason and rationality as historical that prioritized for him the need to "analyze forms of rationality": this meant analyzing the "different foundations, different creations, different modifications in which rationalities engender one another, oppose and pursue one another."[6] Instead of accepting reason and rationality as if they are ahistoric or atemporal, universal features of objective reality, Foucault believes that we have to work at "isolating the form of rationality presented as dominant" at any given time and

[4] Prado 2008, 91, Rhem 2006.
[5] Foucault, Michel, 1988, "Critical Theory/Intellectual History." Kritzman, Lawrence D., ed., *Michel Foucault: Politics, Philosophy, Culture: Interviews and Other Writings 1977–1984*, Oxford: Blackwell's, 17–46, 28.
[6] Foucault 1988, 29.

in any given context, and which then is "endowed with the status of the one-and-only reason." The objective of this isolation, this circumscription, is "to show that it is only *one* possible form among others."[7]

The idea that reason and rationality are historical, that they are temporally and regionally circumscribed and are the products of incremental developments in various milieus, is one that is often relied upon, if not explicitly articulated, by some who are concerned with questions about elective death. In our time, suicide, assisted suicide, and euthanasia in dire circumstances, especially in terminal illness, are increasingly seen in a more tolerant light by health-care professionals and the general public. We seem to have progressed, or at least changed, from thinking of human life as inviolate to thinking of it as worth maintaining only if it offers satisfactory levels of experience. We now have Belgium and Luxembourg allowing physicians to assist patients in dying as the Netherlands has done for some years; Switzerland and Germany allow assistance in dying in some cases; assisted suicide is legal in Oregon and Washington state; and the Montana Supreme Court is considering whether the state constitution protects assistance in dying.

Additionally, and perhaps ultimately more important, is that there has been a notable change in physicians' attitudes away from thinking it to be their professional duty to keep their patients alive as long as is humanly possible. Neither the legitimization of assistance in dying nor the change in physicians' attitudes would have come about without a significant shift in people's ways of thinking about the value of life and the possible desirability of death under certain circumstances. This shift in priorities and attitudes is due to contemporary conceptions of life, death, morality, and experiential value having evolved significantly from older ones, largely due to a lessening of religion's grip on people's thinking and to an increasingly realistic grasp of the nature of the survival enabled by historically recent advancements in medical techniques.

For many the shift in attitudes toward life and death is wrong or at least suspect. In particular, cynics argue that the turn toward greater acceptance of elective death, which is usually painted as a maturing of our attitudes toward life and death, is hypocritical because it is due

[7] Foucault 1988, 27.

only to a congruence of an unsustainable health-care system, dwindling resources, and the escalating financial cost of keeping the sick and the very old alive.[8] Where postmodernism comes in is that some maintain that there is no question of the new attitudes to life and death being wrong or suspect; they simply are different and as legitimate now as their predecessors were thought to be in their times.

This is the core of the postmodern view: there are no extraperspectival standards or criteria by which particular perspectives may be judged. It was not Foucault but Richard Rorty who most succinctly captured this point. Rorty maintained that there is "no criterion that we have not created in the course of creating a practice"; there is nothing that determines our judgments "that is not obedience to our own conventions."[9]

With respect to our particular concern, the challenge to the rationality principle implicit in postmodernist claims is that the shift in attitudes toward so fundamental a matter as elective death both illustrates and is legitimized by how reason and rationality are products of changing intellectual conceptions and practices. The counter to this view is that the shift actually illustrates increasing clarity and effectiveness in how we reason about life and death, and hence marks a move to a more rational approach to life and death. The point here, in more general terms, is that claims about the historical nature of reason and rationality can always be responded to with counterclaims about the better or at least different employment of ahistorical reason and rationality. Moreover, the availability of ready recourse to the application of reason and rationality when their nature is questioned suggests what actually is the case, which is that reason and rationality are not products of thought but are conditions of thought. This brings me to what I believe is the most effective rebuttal to Foucauldian and postmodern conception of reason and rationality as historical products of different intellectual and practical milieus.

Hilary Putnam spoke for many philosophers and others when he argued against postmodernists, and relativists generally, that

[8] Caplan, Arthur. 1981. "The 'Unnaturalness' of Aging – A Sickness Unto Death?" Arthur Caplan, H. Tristram Engelhardt, Jr., and James J. McCartney, eds., *Concepts of Health and Disease*. Reading, MA: Addison-Wesley, 725–737.

[9] Rorty, Richard, 1982, *The Consequences of Pragmatism*, Minneapolis: University of Minnesota Press, xlii.

historical standards and developments "cannot define what reason is" because historical standards themselves "presuppose reason...for their interpretation."[10] This particular contention is effective in that by stressing the presuppositional role of reason, it poses for postmoderns the extremely difficult question as to what devices or criteria are employed in determining or trying to determine that reason and rationality are historical in nature. The contention has the effect of pushing postmoderns – and Foucault – into a position they often end up occupying, namely, a radical relativism that simply levels the playing field by making every view as good as every other.[11] In the particular case, if all standards are historical and there are no objective standards or criteria by which to determine the historicity of reason or of anything whatsoever, the claim that reason and rationality are historical either is rendered empty of content or its claimants tacitly acknowledge that it is all a matter of how individuals or groups prefer to think about reason and rationality.

But Putnam goes deeper. Aside from arguing that interpretation of historical standards presupposes reason, so reason cannot itself be historical, he points out an even more basic conceptual fact, which is that rationality is "a regulative idea" that governs all cases of debate, assessment, and inquiry, and which thus enables us "to criticize the conduct of all activities and institutions."[12] Putnam's persuasive point is that reason and rationality, like truth and knowledge, are and must be prior to inquiry, assessment, and debate.

Foucault was well aware of Putnam's view as it was articulated by various thinkers. He was especially conscious of Putnam's view as it was used to ground several critiques of his own thought and work. In response, Foucault charged those who take Putnam's side with "blackmail." That is, Foucault claimed that those who see reason and rationality as ahistorical, as conceptually prior to any exercise of critical thought, react to "every critique of reason or every critical inquiry into the history of rationality" by imposing a falsely exclusive

[10] Putnam, Hilary, 1987, "Why Reason Can't Be Naturalized." Baynes, Kenneth, James Bohman, and Thomas McCarthy, eds., *After Philosophy*, Cambridge, MA: MIT Press, 222–244, 227.

[11] Krausz, Michael, ed., 1989, *Relativism: Interpretation and Confrontation*, Notre Dame: University of Notre Dame Press, 1.

[12] Putnam 1987, 228.

dichotomy. The supposedly imposed dichotomy is, in Foucault's terms, that "either you accept rationality or you fall prey to the irrational."[13] In other words, Foucault saw criticism of his views on reason as more normative than analytically critical, as relegating all challenges to established understanding of reason as outright rejection of reason.

Foucault's response is flawed in two ways that are characteristic of his responses to criticism of his position. The first way is also characteristic of responses by other postmoderns to criticism of their claims and is that Foucault ignores or possibly fails to see the complexity of Putnam's position. Part of the complexity is that Putnam and anyone agreeing with him can accept the ahistorical nature of reason and rationality without precluding the raising of critical questions about their application. For instance, questions may be raised about how use of reason may be colored by ideology without implying that reason is a product of ideology. Additionally, accepting reason and rationality as ahistorical certainly does not preclude critical inquiry into the history of how reason and rationality have been applied and understood in different historical eras. The possibility of such inquiry seems to allow everything Foucault wants to do with respect to analyzing the "different foundations, different creations, different modifications in which rationalities engender one another, oppose and pursue one another."[14] All that is necessary is to understand Foucault's reference to "rationalities" as reference to the various historical ways rationality is described and employed rather than to separate and distinct rationalities.

Putnam says nothing preclusive about examining how reason and rationality may have been differently understood at different times or in different intellectual contexts: for instance, as gifts of God or as Platonic essences or as an exclusively masculine property or as racially contingent. Nor does Putnam preclude that reason may have been systematically misused in certain specific ways in various epochs, for example by employment of religious or other dogmas as unquestionably true premises in supposedly well-reasoned arguments and contentions. Putnam's point has to do with how reason and rationality's fundamental principles, such as noncontradiction

[13] Foucault 1988, 27.
[14] Foucault 1988, 29.

and inferential validity, cannot be adopted and discarded, qualified and modified, depending on historical, ideological, and social contexts because they are not the products of social, ideological, and historical developments.

It is notable that I have never encountered a postmodern argument to the effect that numbers are historical constructs and that seven and five being twelve is a contingent matter and variable depending on social and historical context. To be sure, there are debates between realists and nominalists about the nature of numbers, but they all count, add, and subtract in the same way. There definitely has been progress, and therefore historical change, in numeration, most notably when Arabic numbering introduced the zero that was lacking in Roman numbering. But recognition and representation of nullity was not invention of nullity. What would it be to maintain that simple addition or subtraction is historically contingent? Similarly, what would it be to reject and to be "right" in rejecting the law of noncontradiction depending on social, ideological, or historical context? Again, there has been progress, and thus historical change, in understanding of reason, most notably when Aristotle "codified" basic aspects of reasoning in his logic, thereby clarifying and systematizing what was previously imprecise. But as with the case of nullity, articulating that if all As are Bs, and C is an A, then C is a B, was not the invention of something new; it was recognition of something inherent to rational thought.

The comparison of reason and rationality with numeration brings out more strongly the point made earlier about the difference between making contentions about reason and rationality's nature being historical and making contentions about their historical application. The comparison also brings out how there is something amiss in considering reason and rationality in terms of their nature, as Foucault in effect does in arguing that they have a different nature than traditionally thought. The point, which is clear in Putnam's arguments, is that reason is a capacity, as is rationality in some uses; in other uses rationality is a trait or attribute.

Reason is normally defined as either practical or theoretical. Practical reason is typically defined as "the capacity for argument or demonstrative inference, considered in its application to ...

prescribing or selecting behavior."[15] Theoretical reason is defined as a "capacity whose province is theoretical knowledge or inquiry; more broadly, the faculty concerned with ascertaining truth of any kind."[16] Rationality is typically defined as "a normative concept" understood as referring to a capacity or attribute determining that "for any action, belief, or desire, if it is rational we ought to choose it." Rationality also is defined as "a descriptive concept" understood as referring to "those intellectual capacities ... that distinguish persons from plants and most other animals."[17] Theoretical and practical rationality are defined very much as are theoretical and practical reason.[18]

Reason, as a capacity, is not historical and it is, in fact, difficult to see what sense we might give to it or any capacity being "self-created" if being historical means that it would be a capacity somehow established or produced by practices that would in themselves be exercises of that capacity. We can readily enough imagine an inchoate and perhaps unrecognized capacity being developed, as reason might be gradually honed in being applied, but practices cannot generate capacities. Rationality, as either a capacity or an attribute also is neither historical nor self-created. What can be historical, and thus be isolated as the "dominant" form of rationality, is how the capacity or attribute is conceived of at a particular time – for instance, as a gift of God. What can be historical, and be "endowed with the status of the one-and-only reason," is how reasoning principles are articulated and applied at a given time. But if Foucault's is not to be only a sociohistorical claim, if it is to be a claim challenging the philosophical conception of reason and rationality, it must go deeper and contest reason and rationality as Putnam describes them: as conditional capacities. For his to be a philosophical claim, Foucault has to challenge and significantly impugn Kant's point that reason and rationality are conditional to inquiry as temporality and cause/effect are conditional to conceptualization of the world.

---

[15] Audi 1995, 636.
[16] Audi 1995, 796.
[17] Audi 1995, 674–75.
[18] Audi 1995, 675; see also *Stanford Encyclopedia of Philosophy*, 2009a, *http://plato. stanford.edu/search/searcher.py?query=reason.*

The second flaw in Foucault's position regarding reason and rationality's alleged historical nature needs little discussion and is that he exaggerates how Putnam and others allegedly respond to historicist critiques of rationality and reason by dismissing them as irrational. In the article quoted earlier, Putnam argues cogently and carefully against historicist critiques and interpretations of reason and rationality, which he would hardly bother to do if he did, as Foucault alleges, dismiss historicists and postmoderns as irrational. In arguing as he does, Putnam is not only preaching to the converted; he precisely is using reason to expose the errors in thinking that reason and rationality are by nature historical products. Briefly put, what Putnam is saying is that to evaluate how reason and rationality are and have been understood and used, one needs to reason in order to proceed in a sound, productive, and precisely rational manner. Moreover, one needs to presuppose rationality both in order to take one's own thinking and conclusions seriously and as reliable, and to expect that others will follow one's thinking, whether or not they ultimately accept one's conclusions. Admittedly, there are philosophers and others who dismiss postmodern views as irrational, but Putnam's contribution to the debate is not a dismissive one, nor does he impose some extreme and preclusive dichotomy. What he does is offer a carefully thought-out argument directed at opponents he takes seriously but whom he sees as failing to appreciate – or perhaps understand – the conditional or presuppositional nature of reason and rationality.

What I have described as the postmodern challenge specifically affects application of the rationality criterion in two different but related ways. One is that postmodern critiques of reason and rationality cannot be ignored when there is significant recourse to reason and rationality conceived of as ahistorical and applying equally to everyone. Assuming that the foregoing discussion and recourse to Putnam's argument deal with the general postmodern challenge to universalist conception of reason and rationality, or at least do so sufficiently for our present purposes, we need to acknowledge the other way the challenge impacts on the criterion. This other way is that assessments by electors of their own elective-death decisions, and survivors' assessments of electors' decisions, are unquestionably colored not only by their feelings and emotions, but also by their religious or metaphysical and other deep-seated beliefs as well as their cultural and personal values. As a consequence, electors' and survivors' assessments may well be more or less slanted by greater or lesser subordination of their reasoning to their beliefs, values, and feelings.

What poses the biggest problem about this subordination is that electors and survivors are rarely aware that their assessments of electors' decisions are colored by their feelings, values, and especially deep-seated beliefs. For them, it is often simply a matter of the decisions either making sense or not making sense. Most often, survivors assess electors' decisions mainly by putting themselves in electors' place and determining what they themselves would do. It is this perspective-centeredness that the postmoderns draw on most successfully in posing their challenge. The postmodernist contention is that if the decisions are perceived as sensible or otherwise, whether by electors or survivors, there are no grounds on which to maintain that despite appearances, the decisions are other than as perceived and that they would be seen to be so were it not for the roles of beliefs, values, and feelings.

As usually articulated, in more or less sophisticated terms, the contention is that if values, feelings, and beliefs are what define individuals as the persons they are, and thus determine their assessments of elective-death decisions, then there is no sense to the idea that we should – or can – have recourse to objective criteria according to which the decisions might emerge as other than as seen by electors and survivors and any others concerned with electors' choices to die. It is this second way that the postmodernist challenge impacts on the rationality criterion that connects the first and the second philosophical challenges and poses a serious question for what I have argued.

THE SECOND CHALLENGE

We come now to the second philosophical challenge to the rationality criterion as presently formulated. As noted at the beginning of this chapter, the challenge was articulated by Battin in terms of my needing to consider the "secular skeptic's concerns about religions' claims for the possibility of an afterlife, and whether this person's choices about suicide can be rational if he or she fails to acknowledge that death may *not* be annihilation."[19] Initially it is easy to think that all that is needed to deal with Battin's point is to include reference in the criterion to acknowledgment that death may not be personal annihilation. Unfortunately, such emendation of the rationality criterion would prove seriously insufficient.

The trouble is that Battin's point raises the broader question of what can be expected regarding electors acknowledging either that death may be personal annihilation or that it may not be annihilation. The point of including the required acknowledgment that death may be annihilation in the rationality criterion was to prevent electors' assuming that in ending their lives they would only be ending their earthly existence and would survive, as themselves, in some other state or plane of being. To end one's life on the basis of this conviction, a conviction that however strong it may be remains unproven and unprovable, is not rational because to do so is to take as factual something that is only a belief, and at that a belief with no hard evidence supporting its truth.

Much of the force behind requiring acknowledgment of the possibility of annihilation is the fact that belief in an afterlife is an historically persistent one and a very widely held view. Additionally, some argue that among the chaff of television programs about ghost-hunters, mediums' persistent claims, numerous stories about apparitions, and a vast otherworldly literature, there is some serious evidence that perhaps we do survive physical death.

Battin's expressed concern is that there is another side to the coin of individuals choosing to die firmly believing that they will survive death as persons, which is individuals choosing to die firmly believing that death is personal annihilation. I have argued that the former are acting irrationally because they are relying on unconfirmed beliefs as factual premises or as factual parts of their motivation. Battin rightly points out that individuals choosing to die without considering that there may be an afterlife may also be acting irrationally, and for the same reasons. It is not hard to see the force of her concern because it is conceivable that individuals choosing to die may not only survive as persons, but may be punished for taking their lives or, as Battin

---

[19] Battin 2009.

pointed out to me, perhaps they may be rewarded for facing the ends of their blighted lives courageously.[20] These individuals, then, would be acting irrationally if they do not consider the possibility of an afterlife. However, as alluded to above, once Battin's concern is articulated, it becomes insufficient to simply further amend the rationality criterion by adding acknowledgment of the possibility of an afterlife as a requirement. For one thing, mere inclusion of the need to acknowledge that death may not be annihilation, like inclusion of the acknowledgment that death may be annihilation, would run counter to deeply held and often carefully thought-out views on the finality of physical death. It is this cognitive resistance to both acknowledgments that poses the broader question raised by Battin's concern.

The broader question is less a question about conceivable possibilities regarding the actuality of an afterlife or annihilation than it is about electors, and survivors' capacities. The capacities I mean are those of both believers in an afterlife and Battin's secular skeptics to consider possibilities profoundly contrary to their beliefs in an authentic and genuine manner. If individuals are the persons their beliefs, values, and practices make them, it may well follow that they as persons are psychologically or even conceptually unable to make the required acknowledgments because to do so is to incorporate a measure of doubt about an afterlife or annihilation into their thinking about elective death, and hence to qualify or even jeopardize the consistency of their very being as persons.

Consider once more the case of the king's horseman, and imagine talking to him about his decision and trying to get him to consider that his belief in an afterlife in which he continues to serve his king is one he must question or at least not take for granted in deciding to end his life. The horseman's case is illustrative because if he does manage to authentically acknowledge that the afterlife he believes in – a rather specific sort of afterlife – may not exist, then his decision to end his life to continue serving his king simply makes no sense. Without his felt-certainty that his death is transition to another realm where his dead king waits for him to continue his service, the horseman's killing himself to continue serving his king reduces to

[20] Personal correspondence.

him ending his life only for the possibility of doing so. This means that the horseman authentically acknowledging that death may be annihilation is for him to in effect change his purpose in taking his own life. Here we have what makes the horseman's case particularly illustrative: the specific nature of his belief in an afterlife renders acknowledgment of the possibility that death is annihilation equivalent to a change of objective in committing suicide. The acknowledgment, then, is highly significant for the horseman, and given the integration of his belief with everything else that defines him as a person, it is not only unlikely that the horseman would be willing or even able to make the acknowledgment, and if he did, he might not fully grasp what it amounts to.

What needs to be appreciated here, and what most closely connects the two philosophical challenges to the rationality criterion, is that what we are actually dealing with are not particular beliefs about either an afterlife or the finality of physical death.[21] Rather, we are dealing with holistic EONs; we are dealing with experience-organizing narratives or what I described in Chapter 1 as perspective- and attitude-determining latticeworks of beliefs, values, and practices. The point here can be made by noting that the horseman's EON, the way he makes sense of his life, his world, and his very existence, incorporates in a fundamental way credence in a life-and-death cycle in which his earthly death is a transition to another form of continuing to be the person he is. The point, then, is just this: how can application of the rationality criterion presuppose and indeed require that the horseman put aside his EON and authentically consider that ending his life may actually be annihilating himself as a person?

Another complication evident in the horseman's case is that the entertaining of doubt about the afterlife may be forbidden by the doctrines of his religious faith. To see the force of this point, consider that some religions – notably Islam and Catholicism – forbid the very entertaining of doubt about God's existence or other fundamental doctrines and consider doing so a grievous and punishable fault. What is of greatest relevance to us regarding such prohibitions is that as well as positive inclinations, the horseman's EON will include

---

[21] See the Appendix for a detailed discussion of the complexity of belief in an afterlife.

negative elements strongly predisposing him to avoid doubt of the relevant sort, and to him being asked to make the acknowledgment about the possibility of annihilation would decidedly sound to him as being asked to doubt a key aspect of his faith.

The issue that emerges in considering these two challenges, then, is one about the degree to which the horseman can make the acknowledgment of the possibility that death is annihilation as required by the rationality criterion. This is a question about the degree to which such an acknowledgment, if made, can be meaningful if it runs counter to everything the horseman's EON or experience-organizing narrative determines to be his reality, as well as runs counter to his faith's specific demands and prohibitions.

While the horseman's case is one of someone who believes in an afterlife and is particularly useful here, it is not difficult to produce a parallel case in which a secular skeptic's EON would be as intolerant of acknowledgment of the possibility of an afterlife as the horseman's EON is intolerant of acknowledgment of possible annihilation. The following is the case of someone known to me personally and I use it because unlike other cases I know of, it is lacking the sort of possibly dubious psychological mechanics that often characterize breaks with religion and abandonment of belief in an afterlife. I will call the person in question Michael, without necessarily implying anything about gender.

Michael was raised a Catholic, attended Catholic grade school, and served as an altar boy through his sixth, seventh, and eighth grades. Michael enjoyed a strong faith into his early twenties. At twenty-five he married a woman who had also been raised a Catholic but who abandoned religion when she finished school, went to work, and left her parents' home. What complicated her abandonment of religion, as is fairly typical of such cases, was that she had a bitter falling out with her mother for giving up her Catholicism. She did, however, respect Michael's commitment to the Church and certainly understood it. For his part, Michael never discussed religion with his wife.

Shortly after their marriage, Michael and his wife traveled abroad and worked for a time in another country. As it happened, there was a Catholic church almost directly across the street from where the couple was living, which facilitated Michael continuing to attend Sunday Mass and occasionally other services. However, he soon found himself turning up for Mass later and later and then began leaving early. He also stopped going to other services, particularly going to confession. Finally, one Sunday when he had arrived late to Mass and had simply stood just inside the door of the church, he found himself turning to leave little more than halfway through the service. Michael then examined his motives and in a surprisingly calm way realized that the service no longer meant anything to him, that he no longer understood why he was attending, and that doing so had become pointless. He left the church and did not return.

What makes Michael's case interesting for us is that he gave a lot of thought to the possibility of an afterlife detached from religious doctrines. He read a number of books on the topic, including some by areligious scientists claiming that survival of death is possible in purely physical terms, such as through preservation of brain waves as electrical patterns. Ultimately, however, he found that the notion of an afterlife had become as meaningless for him as had religion. It is this meaninglessness that poses the question here of how authentically Michael could acknowledge the possibility of an afterlife in considering elective death. At present Michael has lived as one of Battin's secular skeptics for over forty-five years, compared to the roughly eighteen or twenty years he lived as a knowing Catholic. Michael's EON now simply has no room for the possibility of an afterlife, so any acknowledgment he might make of that possibility would be a *pro forma* one and almost certainly fall short of what the rationality criterion requires. The meaninglessness of the idea of an afterlife in Michael's case illustrates how it may prove even more difficult for a thoroughgoing skeptic to authentically acknowledge the possibility that death is not personal annihilation, than for someone who believes in an afterlife to authentically acknowledge the possibility that death is annihilation.

Note that in considering the case of the skeptic we are not limiting ourselves to atheists who, in denying the existence of God also deny the existence of an afterlife. For one thing, belief in an afterlife need not entail belief in God, just as belief in God need not entail belief in an afterlife. Nor are we dealing only with atheists and agnostics, where the latter simply reserve judgment about God and an afterlife. We are also dealing with individuals like Michael, whose EON simply disallows either or both of the notions of a God and of an afterlife as meaningful ones. But in all cases where an afterlife is denied or the idea of it found vacuous, it is difficult to see what acknowledgment of the possibility of an afterlife would come to. Worse, it could be argued that the criterion's required acknowledgment actually is counterproductive in that it undermines the rationality of skeptics' elective-death decisions by evoking from them what would be essentially empty concessions. Moreover, the same is true of acknowledgments of the possibility that death is annihilation wrung from electors who do believe in an afterlife.

Battin's challenge, then, leaves us needing to reconsider the question of whether rational elective-death deliberations and decisions have to – or can – require acknowledgment that there may or may not be an afterlife.

RESPONDING TO THE CHALLENGES

We seem to be in or at least dangerously close to the position of having to grant that the soundness of elective-death reasoning is considerably more a function of individual EONs than it is of universal standards. In other words, the combined effect of the implicit postmodern challenge to the rationality criterion, and of Battin's explicit challenge regarding the rationality of elective death decided on without consideration of the possibility of an afterlife, seems to be that elective-death reasoning cannot be assessed and judged solely on the basis of universal standards for reasoning validity. There seems to be need to assess elective-death reasoning more as the criterion requires that elective-death motivation be assessed. It appears that electors' EONs must be taken into account with respect to their reasoning about choosing to die, just as they must be taken into account with respect to their motives for choosing to die. If this is the case, the postmodern challenge in effect succeeds, and it does so in an ironic manner: it succeeds, not as intended by impugning the universality of reasoning standards, but rather by showing their insufficiency.

At least since Aristotle we have thought of ourselves as rational animals, as beings defined by reason and rationality. We designate ourselves, as a species, as *homo sapiens*, a phrase that in Latin means "wise man" and characterizes us as differing from other animals in virtue of our being rational. But our EONs have more to do with defining each of us as individuals than does a shared rationality, and our EONs are composed not only of reasoned conclusions but also a mélange of beliefs, values, lasting impressions, affective dispositions, and more than a few illusions. The inconvenient truth is that if we assess our own or others' reasoning strictly by logical standards, we invariably get things wrong if only because of incompleteness. The rationality criterion attempts to deal with this fact by requiring different assessments of reasoning and of motivation. However, that approach works well enough only until we encounter the problem of individuals' incapacities to factor certain elements effectively into their reasoning.

When electors or survivors need to think hard about elective death, the chances are high that they will have what Alisdair MacIntyre called "epistemological crises."[22] These are situations where individuals find themselves forced to question what they previously accepted unquestioningly. What makes MacIntyre's epistemological crises special is that the extremely problematic situations individuals face do not only force questions about particular matters but also about the judgment standards they previously used to solve such matters. Epistemological crises occur when individuals face the need to make a decision or resolve an issue that confronts them and they find that the standards they have always used to make decisions or resolve issues are themselves impugned by what confronts them. In other words, individuals may find themselves at a loss as to how to resolve perplexities because the ways they normally have resolved perplexities are put into question by the perplexities they face.

To summarize the problem, it is that strict application of the rationality principle is very likely to prompt epistemological crises not only in electors, but also in survivors who do or do not believe in an afterlife. The reason is that if electors' and survivors' EONs incorporate deep-seated beliefs that there is an afterlife or that physical death is personal annihilation, and application of the rationality criterion requires them to authentically and seriously entertain the idea that their beliefs may be wrong, the unintended effect basically is to deprive these individuals of an established component of their

---

[22] MacIntyre, Alisdair, 1977, "Epistemological Crises, Dramatic Narrative and the Philosophy of Science," *The Monist*, 60(4), 453–472.

decision-making and issue-resolving dispositions and practices. In addition, it is to in effect destabilize beliefs and related values that at least in part define them as the persons they are.

Should we therefore admit that the role of individuals' EONs is so fundamental to how they function as thinking beings that we cannot expect believers in or skeptics about an afterlife to reason about elective death as the criterion requires? Must we remove from the criterion the requirement that death be acknowledged to possibly be annihilation, and refrain from adding a companion requirement that the possibility of an afterlife be acknowledged?

To proceed, I need to briefly review what I have been trying to establish and can offer no more succinct summation than is given by Battin in her review of *Choosing to Die*. She tells us that, on the one hand, "*yes*, suicide can be rational if elected in a clear-thinking, voluntary way, without pressure or undue influence, external or internal, and with full information," or, on the other hand, "*no*, suicide is irrational, since it may be based on a narrow, pessimistic view of one's future, on short discounts and high emotionality, or because it fails to recognize the impossibility of discerning what (if anything) comes after death."[23] The rationality criterion is supposed to serve as a device to determine that the conditions Battin lists on the positive side are met. However, it seems that the presently required acknowledgment of the possibility death is annihilation, and the potentially added requirement of acknowledgment that there may be an afterlife, raise the question of how authentic the required acknowledgment or acknowledgments could be if wholly at odds with electors' EONs.

What I want to propose is that short of making rational decisions and acts entirely contingent on individuals' EONs, the only way out of the predicament regarding the rationality criterion's requirements and individuals' possible incapacity to authentically acknowledge the possibility of annihilation or an afterlife, is to shift the place of belief or disbelief in an afterlife in assessment of elective-death consideration and decisions from the reasoning side to the motivation side of the assessment.

[23] Battin 2009.

There are two advantages to the proposed shift of the afterlife/annihilation question from reasoning to motivation. The first is that it recognizes that where belief in an afterlife or in annihilation plays a prominent role in consideration of elective death, it actually operates as a premise or accepted fact in reasoning only in a derivative way. What I mean by this is that if an elector's choice to die is based to a greater or lesser extent on belief in an afterlife or in annihilation, the belief in question is not a separate element in reasoning but usually is part-and-parcel of a motive: to rejoin a deceased spouse; to be done with an existence that has lost its attraction. Therefore, multicultural dialogic discussion of the belief-cum-motive will prove considerably more effective than simple requirement of – likely inauthentic – acknowledgments that there might or might not be an afterlife. The second advantage is that by shifting the afterlife/annihilation question to the motives side of assessment of rationality, we preserve the transparency and integrity of assessment of reasoning by limiting it to application of straightforwardly universal standards or principles. It seems, then, that we need to further emendate the rationality criterion, but not by adding a further requirement regarding acknowledgment of the possibility of an afterlife. Instead, the emendation shifts consideration of what electors believe about death's consequences to the motives side of the criterion. As will emerge, this change not only answers Battin's concern, it produces an intuitively clearer formulation of the rationality criterion.

Recall that the last formulation of the rationality criterion, criterion E, was as follows:

Self-killing is rational if autonomous, soundly reasoned, adequately informed, includes acknowledgment death may be personal annihilation, and multicultural assessment determines it best serves one's interests while timed to least harm survivors.

As noted earlier, the elements of the criterion are: (i) autonomous choice, (ii) sound reasoning, (iii) adequate information, (iv) acknowledgment that dying may be annihilation, (v) multicultural assessment of interests/motivation, and (vi) recognition of survivors' interests.

We might have changed "acknowledgment death may be annihilation" to "acknowledge that death may or may not be annihilation," thus adding "or may not be" to (iv), but doing so would have left us with a criterion weakened by indeterminacy. The proposed shift makes confusing additions unnecessary. What I propose, then, is to implement the shift by rephrasing the criterion as follows:

Self-killing is rational if autonomous, soundly reasoned, and adequately informed, and multicultural assessment determines it best serves one's interests while timed to least harm survivors.

Electors' beliefs and expectations regarding what, if anything, follows physical death are now the subject not of strict logical assessment of reasoning but, rather, of dialogic consideration by cultural peers and members of other cultures. Electors' exposure to different perspectives on death, either as transition to another form of existence or as personal annihilation, will better prompt them to reflect on their own beliefs and better alert them to the need to more carefully consider death's consequences than a formal required acknowledgment would have done.

To close this chapter, I need to make a most important point, one prompted by how some readers may react to the foregoing final version of the rationality criterion. The point I need to make is one regrettably missed by a reviewer of *Choosing to Die*; and I say regrettably because missing this point tends to result in wholly unwarranted trivialization of the rationality criterion.[24]

The point is that in philosophizing, as in many other endeavors, the getting there is more constructive and beneficial than the arriving: in philosophizing, how a conclusion is reached is more important than the conclusion itself, which usually is anticipated. Some readers looking at the foregoing reformulated rationality criterion may feel that it now only states the obvious. This is, while not wrong, a serious misconstrual because of two important and closely related aspects of the idea that the getting there is as or more important than arriving.

The first aspect is that in the present context the criterion and its phrasing are less important than the considerations that led to the criterion's final formulation. It was precisely the considerations we went through, which resulted in the criterion's final formulation,

---

[24] Young 2008.

that provide us with a solid theoretical basis for consistent practical treatment of elective-death cases. The second aspect is that it is all to the good if the criterion now looks obvious. It should look obvious once we have worked through the considerations leading to its final formulation. The obviousness manifests what going through those considerations accomplished: the criterion articulates and systematizes what was previously largely piecemeal in both conception and application, being variously objectified and described and diversely employed. It is in no way undesirable or disappointing that the criterion and its requirements now seem obvious. The criterion and its requirements *should* now seem obvious to us. Ludwig Wittgenstein saw this point clearly, remarking of his own work that if he succeeded in saying what he was trying to say, people would eventually wonder why it all needed saying.[25]

CHAPTER SUMMARY

Two philosophical challenges threaten the rationality criterion and its application. One is the postmodern challenge to the universality of reason and rationality, and hence to the universality of assessment standards for sound reasoning and rational action. The other challenge arises from a question about the criterion's required acknowledgment that death may be annihilation and is that individuals' EONs may and very likely do limit their capacities to authentically acknowledge possibilities at odds with those EONs: with the beliefs, values, interpretive inclinations, affective dispositions, and habitual practices that define them as persons.

Though not as conclusive as one might wish, the response to the postmodern challenge to the universality of reason and rationality is that reason and rationality are conditional capacities and are presupposed by all forms of inquiry, evaluative thought, and practical deliberations regarding action. As conditional capacities, reason and rationality cannot be products of culture, ideology, historical factors, or other activities and developments. The misconstrued grain of truth in the postmodern challenge is that application of

---

[25] Wittgenstein, Ludwig, 1980, *Culture and Value*, ed. G. H. Von Wright, trans. Peter Winch, Chicago: University of Chicago Press, 43ᵉ.

reason and rationality is conditioned by culture, ideology, historical factors, and other activities. Additionally, how reason and rationality are conceived, with respect to what is thought to be their objective nature, varies by culture and ideological and historical contexts. In the end, perhaps the strongest point to make against the postmodern challenge is that it is difficult to understand how fundamental principles of reasoning, such as noncontradiction, could be thought to vary temporally, contextually, and even regionally, just as it is difficult to understand how five and seven adding up to twelve could be true in some cultures, historical periods, or ideological milieus and not in others.

Responding to the challenge about EONs precluding authentic acknowledgment of some possibilities is harder. In the present context, the only practicable thing to do is to put aside the general issue and respond to the challenge by shifting the criterion's requirement for acknowledgment about the possibility that there may or may not be an afterlife from the reasoning side of criterial assessment to the motivation side. The point is not to make the acknowledgments a requirement of sound reasoning *per se*, but rather to make serious consideration about an afterlife or annihilation an element of multicultural assessment of elective-death motivation. The expectation is that dialogic treatment of electors' motives will prompt reflection on the afterlife/annihilation question, and that the roles of electors' beliefs and expectations about an afterlife or annihilation at death are best assessed in that manner.

Shifting the acknowledgment from the reasoning side to the motivation side required further emendation of the rationality criterion. In what is now its final formulation, the criterion may appear to some to state the obvious. However, this is, in fact, as it should be because what is of greatest importance are the considerations that we went through to arrive at the final formulation. It is those considerations, more than the criterion itself, that provide us with a basis for thinking about and dealing with elective death in a systematic rather than a too intuition-dependent, case-by-case manner. Furthermore, that the criterion now appears obvious is all to the good because that means that it captures the essence of proper treatment of elective death.

6

Survivors' Responses

Unlike preceding chapters, this one will focus entirely on survivors' construals of electors' choices to die and their consequent responses to those choices. In particular, we have to consider how to best understand survivors' responses to evaluate whether they are likely to be appropriate or inappropriate to electors' decisions, and so may be potentially harmful to both electors and survivors themselves.

Appropriate responses are those that recognize and either support or do not impede soundly reasoned and acceptably motivated choices to die that serve electors' best interests. Responses also are appropriate if they oppose or impede choices to die that in one or another way fail to be soundly reasoned and acceptably motivated or do not serve electors' best interests. Inappropriate responses are those that support or do not impede choices to die that are not soundly reasoned and/or are unacceptably motivated or are against electors' best interests. Responses are also inappropriate if they support or encourage elective death that does not serve electors' best interests. In a secondary way, survivors' responses may be inappropriate if they incur negative psychological and emotional consequences for them because of failure to understand electors' reasoning or motivation, involve feelings of guilt of the sort I consider below, or are driven by unreflective adherence to iconic or coincidental cultural values, beliefs, and practices.

Little or nothing of what follows in this chapter applies directly to electors' own elective-death deliberations and decisions. I mention this at the outset to stave off confusions that might arise when some points made in what follows do apply to electors' reasoning and motivation and that applicability is not pursued. That some points made apply equally to electors' and survivors' thinking is not of immediate relevance.

The moment we begin to evaluate survivors' responses, as when we assess electors' reasoning and motivation, the question arises as to how generously we can and should interpret many of the factors involved in shaping their decisions and actions. As noted earlier, in *Choosing to Die* I devoted a chapter to considering how some latitude must be allowed in applying the rationality criterion to electors' choices to die.[1] But while it included references to assessments and judgments by others than electors, the treatment of latitude in that chapter was only incidentally concerned with survivors because it dealt with everyone who found themselves needing to determine whether electors were acting rationally in order to respond accordingly to electors' decisions. My aim in "Assessment Latitude," the chapter in *Choosing to Die*, was to offer a more practical account than in the previous chapters of the criterion's actual application, given electors' inevitable deterioration and other considerations affecting their individual circumstances.[2]

In considering survivors' responses, we need to look again at the matter of latitude, not because of electors' mental and physical conditions, but because of how survivors' affective states and EONs condition their perceptions and thinking about their spouses', partners', relatives', or friends' decisions to end their lives. This is necessary because of how their responses affect electors; it is also necessary because of how survivors' responses may have negative psychological consequences in their own lives. The objective, then, is not to establish that survivors' responses to electors' choices are fully rational and that their motivation, where relevant, is acceptable. After all, it is not survivors who are choosing to die. The objective, rather, is to understand and evaluate as generously as we can how survivors' responses are formed. Allowing latitude in assessment of electors' thinking and decisions latitude was called for because

---

[1] Battin 2009.
[2] Prado 2008, 158–78.

of their deterioration; in understanding and evaluating survivors' responses, latitude is called for because of their emotional involvement with electors and by the fact that they must continue living with the consequences of the elective deaths of those closest to them.

The first thing to appreciate is that a factor central to how survivors respond to electors' decisions is time: specifically, how long electors might be expected to live if they do or do not hasten their deaths by refusing treatment or by taking more active steps to end their lives. Objectively, time is of the utmost importance to the question of elective death because as the time left to electors decreases, the deteriorative and practical factors I considered in "Assessment Latitude" begin to overshadow the importance of the strict rationality of electors' decisions. And if electors' deterioration advances enough, the issue of rational elective death becomes moot. At that point survivors are left with no options but to cope with the actuality of what are no longer their spouses', partners', relatives', and friends' elective deaths, but simply their natural deaths as caused by their afflictions. But, more subjectively, what is most important about the temporal factor in the present context is survivors' expectations of how long electors might live if they do or do not forgo treatment or commit suicide or request euthanasia.

The crux of the matter is that there may well be significant differences between how electors and their attending physicians estimate how long they might live with and without treatment, and how survivors construe those estimates. Most likely, survivors will construe the estimates more optimistically than electors themselves and their attending physicians. The reasons for the probable disparity have to do with how survivors' perceptions of electors' situations are influenced by their EONs and affective states. To return for a moment to the case of George and Edith discussed in Chapter 3, George's confidence in the advent of more effective treatment for Edith's condition entailed his having more optimistic – in fact, considerably more optimistic – expectations of how much longer Edith might live than the time allowed by her physician's prognosis. This is not necessarily to say that survivors like George are discounting or distorting physicians' prognoses, though they may be doing so; it is to say that survivors commonly focus on the higher ends of the periods of time prognosticated by physicians. For example, survivors will likely interpret prognoses of six to nine months as really prognoses of nine months to a year or even longer, but prognoses hedged by physicians' caution. Survivors could well be right in so interpreting physicians' prognoses in particular cases, but their interpretations may not only be too optimistic; if they are too optimistic they can result in survivors responding quite inappropriately to electors' decisions.

The centrality of survivors' perceptions of what I will refer to simply as electors' "survival time" may be intuitively clear, but what is not so clear is how to quantify survival time to provide us with a reference point in the discussion that follows. The best I can do is to impose a reasonable but ultimately arbitrary time frame on how survivors see electors' survival time in elective-death cases in order to keep the discussion manageable. Of course, a single day or even a single hour can be of great importance when we are considering elective death from survivors' perspectives. But in order to be able to draw some useful conclusions, we need to mark out a period of survival time that is significant enough in duration to preclude objections that opting for elective death is essentially pointless because of the imminence of natural death. We also need to avoid marking out a period of time that is either unrealistically long in the context of terminal illness, or long enough that it diminishes the seriousness of electors' choosing to die by making elective death look too far off in the future.

After talking with a number of people about the matter, and given the inherent inexactness of medical prognoses and of survivors' interpretations of them, I concluded that a period of two months or sixty days is significant enough perceived survival time to differentiate between expected natural death due to terminal illness and meaningful elective death. Additionally, sixty days are not a long enough period of time to diminish the seriousness of elective-death decisions. We will take it, then, that survivors expecting their spouses, partners, relatives, and friends to survive for two months if they do not forgo treatment, commit suicide, or request euthanasia provides us with a reference point for considering survivors' responses to electors choosing to cut short that expected survival time. Note, though, that this reference point has to do only with survivors. It may well be that electors and attending physicians gauge survival time as shorter than sixty days, but our concern is with the expectations that ground survivors' responses, not what we may describe as more objective estimates.

In deciding on a survival time of sixty days, I am putting aside those cases of elective death – suicide, assisted suicide, or requested euthanasia – where the choice to die is prompted by excruciating pain or some similarly unbearable condition. When that point is reached, as I argued in the "Assessment Latitude" section, the question of the rationality of elective death and application of the rationality criterion become redundant. This is because at that point the rationality of ending horrendous and fruitless suffering becomes self-evident. When this happens, survivors are then faced with situations where their only reasonable response-option is to accept electors' – or in many such cases attending physicians' – decisions to stop life-sustaining treatment.

Perceived survival time of sixty days or more of at least tolerable continued life, then, will provide us with a reference point regarding questions about survivors' responses to electors' choices to die. With this reference point established, a few points need to be made. First, what is and is not tolerable survival time for electors will vary with individuals, but for present purposes that variation is more or less taken care of by the fact that their spouses, partners, relatives, and close friends will be fairly well aware of electors' tolerance levels and hence those varying levels will be automatically factored into survivors' perceptions, assessments, and consequent responses.

Second, for argument's sake we will assume in what follows that the survival time prognosticated for electors does not include anticipated mental deterioration of a serious enough sort to rule out the option of elective death. However, the prognosticated survival time may include physical deterioration that could force recourse to assistance in suicide or requested euthanasia.

A third point is that with respect to survival time significantly longer than sixty days, I argued in *The Last Choice* that preemptive suicide may be rational in some circumstances.[3] That is, it may be rational for electors to choose to die even if they can look forward to several years of continued physically tolerable life. Preemptive suicide may be rational if electors' reasoning about and motivation for elective

---

[3] Prado 1990, 1998.

death have to do with avoiding prolonged survival in which they will be significantly lessened as persons because of the effects of their diagnosed or anticipated conditions – early diagnosis of afflictions like Alzheimer's or ALS being cases in point. Preemptive elective death is not a topic we need to pursue here; I mention it only because of the possibility of someone arguing that if electors' prognoses give them a year or two or even more survival time, the rationality of elective death is precluded. I have had this argument made against my position numerous times, usually combined with appeals to what medical advances may be achieved in the relevant time frame and to individuals' capacities to adjust to even the most trying circumstances. I find the argument and the appeals unconvincing, but will not reiterate my contrary arguments; I refer those sympathetic to the argument and the appeals to *The Last Choice*, especially the second edition.[4]

Having decided on using two months as our survival-period base regarding survivors' perceptions and judgments of electors' decisions, we need to face the hard fact that the complexity of individual survivors' responses is too great to enable us to make much progress without again more or less arbitrarily narrowing the range of factors we will address. We can accomplish the narrowing by considering only a small number of salient factors typical to many survivors' responses.

To make some headway, then, we will consider the fewest particular factors common enough in survivors' responses to characterize the nature of affective and cognitive influences on survivors. To this end, I consulted persons having firsthand hospice and hospital experience with the terminally ill to glean from them what many, if not most, survivors typically exhibit in dealing with their spouses', partners', relatives', and friends' choices to die.

The first thing the material I received made clear is that the nature of survivors' initial reactions to electors' choices to die are significantly dependent on the proposed mode of death. The difference is between elective death decided on and achieved passively by refusal of life-sustaining treatment, and elective death decided on and achieved by suicide, assisted suicide, or requested euthanasia.

[4] Prado 1998.

Refusal of food and water falls into a gray area between passive cessation of treatment and active suicide, so it is best if we put this option aside unless there is specific need to consider it. Also, we need not catalog the range of suicidal methods employed to end life because what matters here is simply that regardless of how electors decide to end their lives, survivors will see them opting for cessation of treatment, and perhaps refusal of food and water, in a much less negative light than they will see them opting for suicide or requested euthanasia. This is also true of attending physicians and others professionally involved with the terminally ill.

The fact is that there is still a sharp line drawn by most people between "letting nature take its course" in terminal illness and suicide or requested euthanasia. As should be clear from most of the foregoing in this book, as well as what I discuss and argue in *The Last Choice* and *Choosing to Die*, I believe this distinction is mistaken, if not confused. If there is life-sustaining treatment available, and individuals deliberately choose to forgo that treatment, they are committing suicide. At most the distinction marks a difference in survival time, rather than a significant difference in intention, conception, or ethical status. In any case, the large majority of cases of elective death in terminal illness are instances of refusal of treatment, so the issue is not a pressing one. The most straightforward way to proceed, therefore, is to limit the following discussion to refusal of treatment unless it is specifically noted that what is at issue is suicide, assisted suicide, or requested euthanasia.

Having asked people working in hospices and hospitals what they found typical in their experience of survivors' responses to electors' decisions either to not begin or to cease life-sustaining treatment, the following were the most productive answers I received. First of all, Amber Sharkey, a licensed clinical social worker with hospice experience, provided the most succinct statement of what others also said about what is typical of survivors' responses to electors choosing to forgo therapeutic treatment. And I say "therapeutic" treatment because my understanding is that patients refusing treatment almost never refuse pain-relieving or tranquilizing medication.

Sharkey wrote that in answering what she thought to be most typical of survivors' responses to their spouses, partners, relatives, or friends choosing to forgo initiation or continuation of treatment, she "would have to say fear. Fear of having to face the inevitable outcome and losing the one they love sooner rather than later. Fear of letting go forever. Fear of abandonment." Sharkey also made a key point that captures how fear, in this sense of dread of loss, underlies many survivors' resistance to electors' decisions. She explained that survivors' fear is driven and shaped by their love and concern for electors, as well as by self-concern, and "it is the fear that blocks them from embracing the notion that no treatment is a viable option."[5] In other words, survivors' fear obstructs, if it does not preclude, survivors' understanding that given dire enough conditions and prognoses, electors may be right to reject medically achievable but pointless continuation of their blighted lives.

This blocking of acceptance of what is an option often obviously preferable to continued pointless suffering connects to something I touch on later and consider more carefully in the next chapter. This is what I believe to be a shift in attitude toward death, a shift that seems to be gaining momentum. The connection is that it could be that the sort of blocking that Sharkey describes may be slowly decreasing in prevalence as a common reaction on the part of survivors.

Sandra Taylor, a recently retired chief ethicist at a large general hospital and coauthor of *Assisted Suicide: Theory and Practice in Elective Death*, observed that some family members are "exhausted" by coping with their relations' terminal illnesses.[6] She explained that because of this exhaustion and the feelings of powerlessness that inevitably accompany it, in many cases survivors' responses are that "if the patient decides to forgo aggressive treatment, the family readily agrees."[7] What most concerned Taylor about this response is that survivors' agreement with electors' decisions to cease treatment, or even their inclination to agree with them, inevitably prompts feelings of guilt. It then becomes necessary for attending ethicists and physicians to alleviate survivors' guilt for agreeing to cessation of treatment by assuring them that they are doing the right thing in the circumstances. However, such assurances may not suffice to prevent guilt from affecting survivors' responses. For instance, some survivors may be prompted to resist electors' decisions, despite having initially

---

[5] Personal correspondence.
[6] Prado and Taylor 1999.
[7] Personal correspondence.

accepted them, because of coming to feel guilty about their initial acceptance.

Jane Warner, an oncology nurse, added to Taylor's point about guilt by describing how in her experience relief and resentment are present in many survivors' responses: relief that the ordeal of electors' terminal illnesses is over or will soon be over, and resentment at the adjustments they have to make in their own lives to deal with electors' situations. Warner observed that the relief and resentment are seldom spoken of and are sometimes unacknowledged by survivors, but that both nonetheless prompt feelings of guilt which often complicate survivors' responses. When the felt-guilt is not acknowledged and masquerades as concern or something else; when the felt-guilt is not acknowledged, and hence cannot be reflected on and dealt with by survivors themselves and others who are evaluating survivors' responses, the most common effect the guilt has is to make survivors more unyielding in their resistance to electors' decisions.

I found it interesting that in the comments I received there was a noticeable paucity of references to suicide as a means of elective death, as opposed to refusal of treatment. This paucity of references reflects what I noted earlier, which is that survivors and many health-care professionals view suicide in considerably more negative terms than they do cessation of treatment. Survivors are much more likely to oppose electors' choices to die if the choices involve suicide rather than passively allowing their illnesses to proceed untreated. The fact that mere cessation of treatment only limits the temporal extent of electors' suffering, rather than ending it promptly, seems not to deter most survivors and attending physicians from seeing suicide as unacceptable. Clearly, regardless of how attitudes toward elective death have become markedly more tolerant, and continue to do so, electors' taking active measures to end their lives in terminal illness is still rare in our society and is neither well received by survivors nor encouraged by physicians and other involved professionals.

In any case, cessation of treatment remains by far the most common way for terminally ill patients to realize their elective-death decisions, and is the method most countenanced, if not actually advised, by attending physicians. Additionally, cessation of administration of so-called "aggressive" treatment is the most common action taken by attending physicians in the face of increasingly hopeless patients' conditions. One worrying point, though, is that cessation of administration of treatment is sometimes done without consulting either patients or their families. I think this is important because it dovetails with what is currently happening, which is that at least in some areas an increasingly tolerant attitude among physicians toward merciful euthanasia is markedly outpacing greater tolerance of self-inflicted or assisted suicide.[8]

I will not pursue the question here, but this development calls to mind Arthur Caplan's concern that "the notion will come that the older and disabled who are expensive should do the responsible thing" and end lives that are burdensome to themselves and others. The attitude Caplan fears could well make it eventuate that expedient euthanasia will become not the solution of last resort, but "the attractive solution of first resort."[9] I think the development also raises the question of how big a role is played in physicians' greater tolerance of euthanasia over suicide by their conscious or unconscious unwillingness to cede control over patients in their care to those patients themselves.

What emerges from the foregoing discussion is that factors typical to many if not all survivors' responses to electors' choices, and hence factors that provide a focus for our discussion of survivors' responses, are (i) hopeful expectations about electors' survival time; (ii) fear of loss, finality, and aloneness; and (iii) felt guilt for accepting or inclining to accept electors' decisions, for feeling relieved at electors' deaths or imminent deaths, and for resenting the effects or electors' situations on survivors' own lives. These are factors that play prominent roles in shaping how many survivors respond to their spouses', partners', relatives', and friends' choices to die, and consequently how they

---

[8] Peritz, Ingrid, 2009, "Majority of Quebec Specialists Favor Euthanasia," *Globe and Mail*, Oct. 14: *http://www.theglobeandmail.com/news/national/majority-of-quebec-specialists-favour-euthanasia/article1322669/*; Les Perreaux, 2009, "Quebec Medical College Cautiously Endorses Limited Euthanasia," *Globe and Mail*, Nov. 4; Arthur Schafer, 2009, "The Great Canadian Euthanasia Debate," *Globe and Mail*, Nov. 6.

[9] Caplan, Arthur, 1996, Interview on "The Kevorkian Verdict"; includes interview with Timothy Quill, courtroom coverage, and film of Kevorkian and individuals he assisted in committing suicide. *Frontline*, Public Broadcasting System (WGBH, Boston), May 14; see also Caplan 1981.

either appropriately or inappropriately support or impede electors' decisions and enactment of those decisions.[10]

It is, of course, important not to oversimplify the various complex factors at work in influencing survivors' perceptions, thinking, and judgments regarding electors' decisions, but by focusing on what is salient in typical cases of survivors dealing with their spouses', partners', relatives', and friends' choices to die, we can understand survivors' responses in a general way that would be extremely difficult, if not impossible to achieve were we to attempt to comprehensively catalog and discuss all of the factors that may be operant in shaping survivors' responses.

As noted, how long electors may be expected to live with or without treatment most likely will look different to survivors than to electors and their attending physicians. The differences may not be great, but their consequences can be significant to the appropriateness and inappropriateness of survivors' responses. In perhaps the majority of instances where electors have chosen to commit suicide, a week or even a day of continued survival may look unbearable to electors but most likely will look precious to survivors. Where electors have chosen only to refuse or to discontinue treatment, survival time will be less definite and partly for that reason look trying to electors but again be valued by survivors. Even if electors and survivors both see a day or a week of continued life for electors as unbearable, they need not do so only because of electors' physical pain or punishing deterioration. Both electors and survivors may see a day or a week of further survival as unbearable because it is that much more time filled with fear and the distress of enduring still more hours of helplessness and apprehension for electors, and for survivors that much more time filled with regret, concern, and especially feelings of impotence in the face of loved ones' hopeless situations. These latter are prominently among the cases Taylor describes as ones where survivors are psychologically and emotionally exhausted by dealing with electors' conditions and decline.

The fact remains, however, that in more cases than not, survivors' perceptions of electors' survival time incorporate hope that there

---

[10] Parker-Pope, Tara, 2009. "Treating Dementia, but Overlooking Its Physical Toll," *New York Times*, Oct. 20, Sec. D, 5.

will be some improvement in electors' conditions, that deterioration will slow or stop, or that more efficacious treatment will become available. Hope is a major factor in determining survivors' expectations of electors' survival time, even though it is often vague and unrelated to specific possibilities. I think it safe to say that electors lose hope about their prospects well before survivors do, and that while generally a positive factor, hope in cases of elective death can be counterproductive and negatively influence survivors' responses to electors' choices to die.

Survivors' too-hopeful expectations of electors' survival time, together with fear and feelings of guilt, result in a potent combination of influences on survivors' behavior in dealing with electors' decisions. However, these hopeful expectations, fear, and feelings of guilt at least are factors specific to survivors' situations regarding electors' choices to die, and their specificity to such situations makes it likely that they will be recognized as operant factors and be addressed by both survivors and especially by those counseling them. Survivors' EONs, by contrast, are not factors specific to elective death cases, but they are every bit as influentially potent as overly optimistic expectations, fear, and guilt.

Whereas survivors' expectations regarding electors' survival time, fear, and guilt directly influence their responses to electors' decisions, survivors' EONs more indirectly but just as effectively affect their responses by shaping the character and strength of their expectations, fear, and guilt. Of course, survivors' EONs also affect their responses directly. The most obvious instances of how EONs directly affect survivors' responses are when survivors' and electors' EONs conflict on key points, as in the hypothetical case of George and Edith. For example, electors may believe elective death to be a rational option while survivors believe it to be an unforgivable sin; again, electors may believe physical death to be annihilation while survivors may believe there is an afterlife in which those who commit suicide are punished for eternity. Short of specific conflicts of this sort, EONs affect survivors' responses by, for instance, heightening or tempering survivors' optimism regarding electors' survival time or facilitating or obstructing appreciation of electors' motives for choosing to die.

Perhaps the most worrying practical problem posed by survivors' EONs is that while their expectations about electors' survival time, their fear, and their feelings of guilt normally are anticipated as problematic influences by counselors, physicians, and concerned friends and relatives helping them to cope, the diverse components of survivors' EONs are seldom properly identified and dealt with. Most important in the present context is that attending physicians, counselors, and others are likely to overlook survivors' coincidental cultures and their particular influences on survivors' responses. An added complication is that in our time much that falls into the category of individuals' EONs is deemed private, privileged, and unaddressable unless initially raised by those being counseled. Anyone advising survivors, therefore, will likely rely on conjecture when they are, in effect if not specifically, dealing with influences arising from survivors' EONs. This is where the differences between iconic and coincidental cultures become most troublesome because the conjecture in question invariably relies too heavily on the relatively evident iconic cultural aspects of survivors' EONs, thereby inevitably leading to neglect of influences arising from coincidental cultural aspects.

A possibly hopeful sign that survivors' EONs are being looked at more closely, even if not under that description, is that recently there has been recognition that survivors' responses pose serious issues in that some difficult-to-isolate factors determining their responses occasionally cause conditions that approach pathological proportions. One such condition that has received attention is "complicated grief" or "prolonged grief disorder."[11] These are cases where survivors are unable to move beyond the immediate effects on them of electors' deaths and perhaps even just of electors' choices to die. Therapy is then required to help affected survivors come to terms with whatever persistent form their grief has taken.

In any case, to adequately understand survivors' responses to electors' choices, we decidedly need to consider the roles of their EONs. It is their EONs that determine survivor's initial perceptions of and reactions to announcement of electors' choices to die, as was illustrated in our discussion in Chapter 3 of George's EON-driven

---

[11] Schumer, Fran, 2009, "After a Death, the Pain That Doesn't Go Away," *New York Times*, Sept. 29, Sec. D1, D6.

resistance to Edith's decisions to stop her treatment and to sanction problematically high doses of pain-relieving medication. Prior to any optimistic expectations about Edith's survival time, and before his having feelings of fear or guilt, George reacted to Edith's decisions with resistance to the idea of her choosing to die and with confidence that better treatment for her condition was or would soon be available. These initial reactions were EON-determined, and they established the character and direction of everything that followed in George's response to Edith's decisions.

Speaking of understanding and especially of the appropriateness and inappropriateness of survivors' responses prompts me to caution readers that while it may sometimes sound like it, I am not in the foregoing or in what follows implying that the rationality criterion is to be applied to survivors' responses to electors' choices to die. The rationality criterion is intended to facilitate assessment of electors' reasoning and motivation. What needs to be done regarding survivors' responses is to elucidate the influences on survivors' responses of their affective states, their iconic and coincidental cultures, and their EONs in order to gain better understanding of their responses. Understanding is necessary to enable dependable and consistent conclusions to be drawn as to whether the responses are reasonable or unreasonable, appropriate or inappropriate in the circumstances. The objective is not to establish that survivors' responses are rational in the same sense that electors' reasoning must be established as sound and their motivation as acceptable. Rather, the objective is to grasp as best we can the nature of survivors' responses and what influences are shaping them.

It may look to some readers as if this objective really is a matter of understanding the psychology behind survivors' responses, rather than something philosophical. If the objective is seen in this way, then it will look as if we are duplicating what trained psychologists and counselors regularly do in treating individual elective-death survivors. But seeing the objective in this way is a misperception because the objective is to understand the kind of conceptual factors operant in determining survivors' responses, not the actual psychological factors operant in individual survivors' reactions to electors' decisions. The objective, therefore, has two component aspects: to articulate the essentially cognitive elements of survivors' EONs influencing their responses, such as George's beliefs about suicide and scientific progress, and to indicate the nature of the affective elements at work in shaping survivors' responses, in particular hopefulness regarding survival time, fear of loss, and feelings of guilt.

It would be difficult to overestimate the importance of survivors dealing appropriately with their spouses', partners', relatives', and friends' elective-death decisions. It is not hard to imagine how inappropriate survivors' responses can result not only in making elective death harder for electors, but in fomenting indecision and in prompting ill-advised actions. And while survivors' inappropriate responses would likely tend to make electors doubt their decisions, it can also happen that inappropriate support for electors' decisions, most often based on cultural beliefs and values, will prompt electors to end their lives when doing so is neither rational nor in their best interests.

In better understanding what is shaping survivors' responses, then, it may be determined that individual survivors are moved by problematic beliefs and values; are misinformed or are drawing invalid conclusions; are being emotionally irrational in one or another way; or that the motives prompting some of their expectations, pronouncements, and actions are self-serving or otherwise questionable. With respect to others than survivors involved in elective death, presiding medical ethicists, attending physicians, and other professionals focus on whether elective death is in electors' best interests in light of their conditions, prognoses, and available treatment options, and whether elective death is ethically and legally permissible in the particular circumstances. As to how their own judgments about elective death are formed, professionals' training and experience provide them with relatively objective bases for evaluating electors' decisions, and most will be familiar with the reliability of prognoses and available treatments and their efficacy. Additionally, professionals have articulated ethical codes to rely on and will know the relevant laws and prohibitions. Although professionals' own beliefs, values, iconic and coincidental cultures, and EONs inevitably color their judgments about electors' choices, unlike most survivors what they actually say and do will be governed by their respective codes. More personally, their training and experience enables them to recognize, temper, and control the effects of their private views of electors' decisions.

Somewhat ironically, when they are assessing electors' choices to die, physicians, ethicists, and other involved professionals are immersed in the practical realities of individual cases and as a consequence they tend to see application of the rationality criterion as at best impractical and at worst pointless. This is regrettable, but I have said enough about the necessity of overcoming this attitude in order to establish a theoretical basis for effective and consistent dealing with elective-death cases. The point here is that contrary to professionals, survivors very likely will see application of the criterion to electors' decisions not only as necessary for electors' sakes, but also as significantly helpful to themselves. They most probably will appreciate how applying the criterion to electors' decisions enables them to form clearer assessments of electors' reasoning and motivation, and so facilitates better sorting out of their own thinking about electors' decisions. Application of the rationality criterion to electors' decisions will reassure survivors that electors' choices to die are autonomous, soundly reasoned, adequately informed, and in their best interests; or application of the criterion will possibly indicate lapses in one or more of these respects. In either case, survivors will be able to respond more appropriately to their spouses', partners', relatives', and friends' choices to die.

Nonetheless, a serious danger arises regarding survivors' EONs and application of the rationality criterion. Some survivors may dismissively preclude application of the criterion by taking the position that electors' elective-death decisions cannot be sound because they presume something unacceptable. The case of George and Edith is again illustrative in showing how this might happen. Recall that the religious component of George's EON initially precluded that Edith could soundly opt for elective death because George firmly believed that suicide is not an option for Edith or for anyone else. For him, Edith's reasoning could not be sound, nor her motivation acceptable, due to both being predicated on a wholly unacceptable premise: that the choice to live or die was hers to make. Moreover, whatever extracultural contributions might have been made in dialogic consideration of Edith's decision would have been beside the point for George if they supported Edith's choice, because his own deep-seated assumption that she did not have a choice about continuing to live ruled out any other perspectives supportive of her decision as based on the same mistake.

The case of George and Edith shows how preclusive responses to elective-death decisions are particularly likely to occur when survivors' EONs are heavily influenced by religious prohibition of elective death. However, preclusiveness need not be a product of religious commitments and beliefs. Some survivors may be unable to countenance electors' choices to die because of secular ethical views about suicide. There also may be emotional or psychological bars, such as feeling deeply that suicide is cowardly and maximally self-demeaning or is abandonment and renunciation of everything survivors hold dear about their relationships with electors.

Preclusion of elective death by beliefs that suicide is divinely or ethically forbidden, or by convictions that it is cowardly or the ultimate violation of interpersonal commitments, indicates how assessment of electors' decisions and evaluation of survivors' responses are very different exercises. With respect to assessment of electors' decisions, the basic question is whether it is rational for them to choose to die; whether it is rational for them to give up irredeemable life to escape the suffering and degradation that continuing to live is certain to bring. But the very fact that this is the focus of assessment means either that nothing in electors' thinking precludes elective death or that they have come to terms with their contrary beliefs about ending their own lives, else the issue of elective death would not arise.

In the case of survivors, the basic question is whether spouses, partners, relatives, and close friends are responding in appropriate ways to electors' choices to die. As we saw earlier, appropriate responses are of two kinds: responses that either support or at least do not impede enactment of electors' rational choices, and responses that discourage or impede electors' choices when those choices are judged to be less than rational. Inappropriate responses are also of two kinds: responses that resist or reject electors' rational choices or responses that accept or encourage electors' less than rational choices. Inappropriate responses may be due to misperceptions or misunderstandings or lack of information, but more commonly they are due to deeply rooted beliefs and values.

Ultimately, survivors' responses to electors' choices are more emotional reactions than they are thought-out ways of dealing with electors' decisions. Certainly survivors' initial responses to electors' decisions are emotional reactions. Thinking out the consequences of the decisions and judging their acceptability invariably follows on prior emotional reactions. Sometimes the initial reactions are confirmed by survivors' thinking about electors' choices; sometimes the initial reactions are tempered or changed. As for the appropriateness or inappropriateness of survivors' responses, the key part played by survivors' expectations about electors' survival time is more important in the thinking out than in the initial reactions, but the expectations themselves tend to be products of those initial reactions, of affective rather than reflective factors.

Roughly speaking, the more survivors care for electors, the more optimistic or at least hopeful their expectations will be. The trouble is that the more optimistic are survivors' expectations, the more they will be inclined to resist electors' decisions to forgo treatment or to take their own lives. Since expectations about electors' survival time tend to form the bases of survivors' responses, if they are overly optimistic or too hopeful and so are out of proportion to electors' actual situations, these expectations are bound to render survivors' responses inappropriate. Nor are survivors' expectations straightforward affective reactions. Fear or dread plays a crucial part in the shaping of these responses in that it is fear that prompts hope or optimism regarding electors' survival time. Unconsciously, fear prompts hope or optimism in a reactive way, and in turn optimistic expectations assuage fear because subjectively they push electors' deaths farther into the future.

Mention of subjective temporal distancing of electors' deaths leads to mention of something else that is of major significance regarding survivors' responses. What I have in mind relates to an aspect of the topic of Chapter 7 and it is not a factor operant in the shaping of survivors' responses like optimistic expectations, fear, and guilt; rather it is more of a phenomenon. When we face a loved one's impending death – and no doubt our own as well – we seem to slip into something like a selective temporal stasis regarding events. What I mean by this is that when we are with the person dying, we somehow take up an attitude or mode of thought and attention that seems to stretch out time, and the closer we are to the person, the more intense this attitude or mode of thought is and the longer it continues.

I recall visiting a friend who was dying, and in talking with her and her husband being struck by how the two of us seemed to zero in on the moment. I remember how it was only as I was leaving, and my friend's husband and I left her room, that the temporal pace picked up as my mind was suddenly filled again with the things I still had to do that day and to a lesser extent the things I had done. In conversation with others, it emerged that they had experienced what I experienced, and that it seemed characteristic of how most of us react to the impending death of someone close. There was general agreement that though this phenomenon feels like time slowing down, it really is a matter of focusing narrowly on the person who is dying and paying no heed to all the things of which we would otherwise be conscious.

There is a parallel here to what one often hears about time slowing down for individuals who find themselves in crisis situations such as in combat and coping with emergencies of various sorts. Again, what happens has less to do with actual temporality than it does with cognitive exclusion of everything except what is immediately pertinent to dealing with whatever is happening. The impending death of a spouse, partner, relative, or close friend is a crisis situation, so it is not surprising that we respond similarly. An added point is that the narrow focusing is highly demanding, and if continued for a time can be very tiring. It seems, then, that this focusing and its maintenance may explain part of what Taylor describes as the exhaustion experienced by family members of the terminally ill.

To conclude, the main problem posed by survivors' inappropriate responses is that if electors have soundly reasoned their way to choosing to die, are properly motivated, and are serving their own best interests, they do not need to have their choices and enactment of their choices made more difficult or obstructed by survivors' unyieldingness regarding elective death. At the same time, survivors' responses cannot be ignored, both because of their close relationships to electors and the seriousness of the consequences to themselves of electors' choices and deaths. Unfortunately, when survivors' responses are inappropriate, not because of misinformation or the like but because of fundamental beliefs and values; because of the nature of their EONs, it is unlikely that counseling and multicultural dialogue will change their minds. The best that can be striven for is to help survivors better understand both electors' reasons for their choices and the bases of their own responses in the hope that better understanding will temper their resistance to or rejection of electors' soundly reasoned and well-motivated decisions.

In those more rare cases where survivors are supporting electors' unsound or wrongly motivated decisions on the basis of iconic or coincidental cultural values and practices, the best that can be done is to expose survivors to different perspectives through multicultural dialogue in an effort to cause them to reflect on their responses and the beliefs and values that underlie them.

What all of this comes to is that as in the case of George and Edith, there is little to be done regarding survivors' inappropriate responses but to counsel them. What poses a difficulty is that while in the case of electors, where what is at issue are their very lives, we have an obligation to assess their reasoning and motivation to insure that they know what they are doing, we have no similar mandate in the case of survivors. Therefore, unless they are coercing electors, all we can do is to talk them through their thinking about electors' decisions to get them to see electors' lack of viable alternatives and the problems with their own responses to their spouses', partners', relatives', and friends' choices to die.

CHAPTER SUMMARY

Survivors' responses to electors' choices to die fall into four categories, two of which comprise appropriate responses and two of which comprise inappropriate responses. Survivors respond appropriately when they accept well-reasoned and well-motivated choices that serve electors' interests. Survivors also respond appropriately when they reject electors' decisions that are not rational in some respect. Survivors respond inappropriately when they accept choices that are not well-reasoned or well-motivated or do not serve electors' interests. And survivors respond inappropriately when they reject electors' well-reasoned and well-motivated decisions that serve electors' interests.

Factors playing crucial roles in survivors' responses are overly optimistic or hopeful expectations about electors' survival time, fear or dread of loss and aloneness, and feelings of guilt. These factors, which are specific to cases where individuals must deal with those closest to them choosing to die, are elusive and difficult to identify and to deal with effectively in particular cases. However, they are familiar as types to and expected by those counseling survivors and therefore will at least be considered and addressed as operant factors.

Not specific to elective-death cases, but as crucial in shaping survivors' responses, are their EONs: their experience-organizing narratives. These include powerful attitude and judgment-determining elements like iconic and coincidental cultural values and beliefs. Because they are not specific to elective-death cases, the influences EONs exert on the forming of survivors' responses may go unrecognized and so unaddressed as operant factors.

In the end, little more can be done regarding survivors' inappropriate responses than to discuss them with survivors with a view to prompting critical reflection on the grounds and causes of how they are responding to electors' choices.

7

Accepting Finality

There has been treatment of philosophical questions about death since at least Democritus, who lived from 460 to 370 B.C. However, the rise of analytic philosophy in the mid and late twentieth century in Britain and North America, and the accompanying disillusionment with metaphysical speculation, strongly tended to limit philosophical treatment of death to purely conceptual questions about the nature, continuity, and end of consciousness and related issues about personal identity.[1] Despite the more-or-less canonical limits on treatments of death, more recently and especially in the past few years there has been an intriguing increase in British and North American philosophers' interest in broader questions about death. Much of the renewed interest is due to the growing importance of work in applied ethics on end-of-life issues, but a number of the more recent books and journal articles go beyond those issues to look at fundamental questions about the nature of human life's inevitable end.[2]

[1] Stanford Encyclopedia of Philosophy, 2009b, http://plato.stanford.edu/entries/death.
[2] Williams, Bernard, 1976, "The Makropoulos Case: Reflections on the Tedium of Immortality," in his *Problems of the Self,* Cambridge: Cambridge University Press, 82–100; Thomas Nagel, 1991, "Death," in his *Mortal Questions,* Cambridge: Cambridge University Press, 1–10; Fred Feldman, 1992, *Confrontations with the Reaper: A Philosophical Study of the Nature and Value of Death,* New York: Oxford University Press; Carlos Eire, 2009, *A Very Brief History of Eternity,* Princeton, NJ: Princeton University Press; Steven Luper, 2009, *The Philosophy of Death,* Cambridge and

More general intellectual interest in the large questions about death has tended and continues to be mainly literary, psychological, and sociological, but works in these areas have also shown a relatively new increase in variously focused considerations of death and how it is approached. The main impetus has been widespread discussion of end-of-life issues, especially assisted suicide and euthanasia: issues that have focused public and learned attention on death and dying.[3]

Increased interest in questions about death is highly significant to our interests, because I believe that the increase marks what I will refer to as a maturing of our thinking about life's end. To make my point, I begin with a quotation from Jacques Choron, who in his useful article on death and belief in immortality observes that a major shift in the predominant attitude toward death occurred when the Renaissance produced a reversal of the previously dominant Greek and especially Christian view of life, a view that cast our earthly existence as little more than a precursor to either the Greeks' dark and ill-defined perpetuity or the Christians' eternal salvation or damnation. Choron remarks that with the advent of the Renaissance, life came to be "not seen any longer as something to be endured but [as] something to be enjoyed and which can be shaped and changed for the better."[4] This was a radical change because it cast human life not as a sort of proving ground for what supposedly follows it, but as something to be treasured for itself and which could be improved with effort and ingenuity.

In my view, the Renaissance view of life is not only still prevalent, it has matured and continues to mature in our time. Somewhat paradoxically, it seems that the more positive view of human life as valuable in itself and not just as precursor to an afterlife, has not only led to attempts to improve the human lot, but eventually enabled a

New York: Cambridge University Press; Todd May, 2009, *Death*, Stocksfield, UK: Acumen.

3   Hamel, Ronald, and Edwin DuBose, eds. 1996, *Must We Suffer Our Way to Death? Cultural and Theological Perspectives on Death by Choice*, Dallas, TX: Southern Methodist University Press; Mullens 1996; Timothy Quill, 1996, *A Midwife through the Dying Process: Stories of Healing and Hard Choices at the End of Life*, Baltimore and London: John Hopkins University Press; Timothy Quill and Margaret Battin, eds., 2004, *Physician-Assisted Dying: The Case for Palliative Care and Patient Choice*, Baltimore and London: Johns Hopkins University Press; Randall and McKim, 2008.

4   Choron, Jacques, 1973, Philip Wiener, ed., *Dictionary of the History of Ideas*, Vol. I, New York: Charles Scribner's Sons, 634–46, 636.

more realistic and objective perception and understanding of death as surcease when good life eventually gives way to blighted life in advanced age or terminal illness.

Mine may be too sanguine a view of the renewed interest in death and of much that has been recently said and written about it, but it does seem that at least as a society, if not yet as a species, we may have matured in our attitudes toward life's inevitable end and are continuing to do so. If I am right about this maturing, if better understanding of and acquiescence to human mortality are indeed growing in scope and depth, then this maturing applies directly to our concerns in the present context because it explains a great deal about the growing acceptance of elective death and even of euthanasia in dire medical situations.

Again if I am right about the maturing regarding death, it appears that there is a more positive and hopeful way of seeing the developments centering around greater acceptance of elective death and of greater reluctance to employ what is known as "aggressive" life-sustaining treatment of moribund patients. These are developments that many view only as dangerous: as a pernicious and essentially self-serving social reaction to a rapidly aging population and to the mounting burdens placed on the medical system by the terminally ill, the very old, and the seriously handicapped. If we are attaining social maturity regarding death, then we need to rethink recent public readiness to accept assisted suicide and euthanasia, rising preparedness on the part of physicians to be evermore sparing in the use of various fairly extreme procedures and treatments, medical professionals' willingness to participate in assisted suicide or engage in euthanasia, and efforts by "death with dignity" groups to support legalization of assisted suicide and requested euthanasia. It may be that these developments actually are – at least in part – the results of a newly gained greater maturity about death and perception of it as surcease from suffering and personal debasement, rather than perception of death as simply as the worst harm that can befall us.

If there is indeed a maturing regarding perception of death taking place in our collective attitude toward it, the impact it may be having on elective-death survivors is no doubt one of moderating the resistance that up to now has characterized how survivors respond to their spouses, partners, relatives, and close friends choosing to die.

Such moderation, if it is indeed occurring, is of major importance to our concern with how survivors cope with electors' choices to die.

Speaking in general terms, the history of intellectual concern with death has been most marked by differences in approaches to death based on varying conceptions of life and its value. Again generally, proposals regarding how to deal with death and our natural fear of it have been of two broad sorts: one centering on advice to think hard and a lot about death: the *memento mori* stance, and the other centering on advice not to think about it at all to the best of our ability.

Still speaking in general terms, history shows that advice to think a lot about death tends to be closely related to a pessimistic view of human life and that because of that close relation thinking about death constitutes "the oldest 'remedy' against the fear of death," which is that diminishment of the value of life proportionately diminishes the threat of its end.[5] This diminishment of life's worth is most evident in Christian portrayal of life as a vale of tears, as a testing or proving ground for eventual eternal salvation or damnation. A similar portrayal, one evident not in religious thought but in the thought of Epictetus and Seneca, casts life as a trial, but not as an antecedent to salvation. Rather, this portrayal casts life as the opportunity to exercise self-discipline and thereby to define one's character and to then accept inescapable annihilation with stoic grace as an essential part of character-definition. As for trying to ignore death and not thinking about it, Michel de Montaigne is one of the more notable individuals to have endorsed this way of coping with the fear of death, but it is a way that is particularly prone to self-implosion because of its complete inability to prevent unpleasant surprises when our own death or that of someone close suddenly becomes imminent.

As implied earlier, the attitude toward death most relevant to our considerations is the one that Choron articulates in saying that "[w]hat usually makes death acceptable is its coming as ... surcease from a life of continuous hardship and particularly from the indignity and suffering of old age."[6] This not only is the attitude that promises

---

[5] Choron 1973, 635.
[6] Choron 1973, 636.

us the best chance of getting survivors to accept electors' choices to die, it is the attitude most compatible with and which must underlie the maturing regarding death that I believe is taking place. This is not an attitude that casts life as a vale of tears, as a precursor to something else; it is an attitude that has as its base the Renaissance view of life as valuable in itself and improvable, but it is an attitude that recognizes that at its end life most often becomes undesirable regardless of how well it has gone previously.

The view of death as surcease is one I relied on heavily in writing *Choosing to Die* and both editions of *The Last Choice*. It is an unfortunate and sad reality that human lives more often than not have hard ends. A quick death during sleep due to an aneurism or something of the sort is what most of us would prefer, but few are that lucky. Whatever one's philosophical views on death and dying, death usually comes as surcease from suffering. This is something survivors must appreciate fully in responding to electors' decisions, and if our views on death are indeed maturing, then there is hope that it is an appreciation that may be becoming easier to achieve for broadly social and cultural reasons as well as purely personal ones.

A good deal of philosophical thinking about death is consideration of whether death is or is not in itself an evil: whether it is or is not always and irrevocably contrary to our interests. Such thinking usually focuses on whether or not death is intrinsically and utterly detrimental to our interests in being our end as living beings and subjects and hence as absolutely precluding for us attainment of any further good. Those who believe in an afterlife reject this focus because they believe that death is a transition and hence not intrinsically harmful because it may make possible attainment of much greater good than is available in earthly life, though of course it also may result in eternal suffering, depending on how life was lived. However, typical philosophical treatments of death tend not to include consideration of an afterlife except as a claimed possibility, and so usually treat the main issue as being whether death is intrinsically harmful as the unqualified end of human consciousness.

Conception and fear of death as the end of conscious existence, as annihilation of the subject, prompted early arguments such as Lucretius' to the effect that death should not be feared because as nonexistence it is wholly irrelevant to us. The arguments usually point out that as we do not lament our nonexistence prior to birth, so we should not lament our eventual nonexistence after death.[7] Epicurus offered a similar argument, maintaining that "the most awful of evils, is nothing to us, seeing that, when we are, death is not come, and, when death is come, we are not."[8] The essential point the arguments make is that when dead, we are no longer subjects; we no longer exist, so the issue of whether death is an evil does not arise. In effect, once we are dead, there is no one, no subject, for whom being dead could be a good or an evil.

Although they may be logical enough, these arguments are seldom convincing. For one thing, the parallel drawn between being dead and not existing prior to birth is beside the point because once we do exist as subjects the situation is a novel one radically different from one of previous nonexistence and one that then does make the reality of eventual nonexistence a possible or likely evil. Epicurus, Lucretius, and like-minded others were no doubt thinking about not fearing the state of being dead, but the state of being dead is not what is at issue. When our own death or that of a loved one is imminent, it is not actually being dead that we primarily fear; it is the dying: what we fear is our lives ending, not their being ended at some future time. In this respect Epicurus and company are right; being dead is nothing to us because there is no "us" when we are dead, but reassurances that being dead is nothing to us rather miss the point and are hardly helpful in dealing with our fear of death in the sense of our fear of dying.

The point is evident when we consider what survivors face and must deal with because what survivors fear is not first and foremost their spouses, partners, relatives, and friends actually being dead in the future, though that is, of course, something they anticipate with great sadness and regret. What they most immediately fear and certainly what they must cope with is those closest to them dying, and especially dying by choice. This is clear in that even if survivors believe in an afterlife, their main concern is the impending earthly death of those closest to them. Epicurus and Lucretius' arguments and others

---

[7] *Stanford Encyclopedia of Philosophy* 2009b; Choron 1973.

[8] *Stanford Encyclopedia of Philosophy* 2009b; May 2009, 23–25, 88–90.

similar to them are of little help to survivors because the challenge they face most centrally has to do, not with the future states of their spouses, partners, relatives, and friends, but with them dying, and deliberately doing so sooner than they otherwise might.

This is the heart of the problem regarding elective-death survivors: they must deal not only with the impending deaths of those closest to them, but also with the stark reality that those closest to them choose to surrender whatever time they have left, and so whatever time they have left to be together, to escape their conditions and worsening prospects. Philosophical arguments or other exercises in thanatology can at best call survivors' attention to aspects of the situations they face that they have overlooked or underestimated or ignored, and that may be all to the good, but at bottom what is necessary is for each survivor to come to terms with the imposing fact that a valued relationships with a close friend or relative, with a partner or spouse, is not only about to end but has been radically altered by the friend or relative, partner or spouse choosing to die rather than to continue to live. This coming to terms is not just a matter of understanding electors' reasons for abandoning life. The hardest part for survivors not only to accept but sometimes even to fully acknowledge, is that a friend or relative or especially a partner or spouse is ready to relinquish life and therefore their relationship to be quit of a punishing and deteriorating existence.

CAN PHILOSOPHY HELP?

Can philosophical treatments of death such as that of Epicurus, which fall short of making a genuine difference to most survivors dealing with elective death, be supplanted with more useful ones? I think they can, and we can do so by taking advantage of a distinction Rorty drew between systematic philosophers like Plato and Kant and edifying philosophers like Gadamer and, in effect, himself.

Rorty observed that "[g]reat systematic philosophers, like great scientists, build for eternity." His point was that those philosophers who are sometimes called "system builders" attempt to provide all-encompassing explanatory schemas of evident and not so evident reality, and that their schemas invariably incorporate complex ontological categories and ethical and aesthetic principles – posited classes of what there is and derived rules for how we should live and what should please us. Contrary to systematic philosophers, rather than offering explanatory schemas "[g]reat edifying philosophers destroy for the sake of their own generation."[9]

It is clear from the context that Rorty might better have said that great systematic philosophers try to build for eternity and inevitably fail, but that is not of immediate relevance; what is of immediate relevance is what Rorty meant by speaking of some philosophers destroying for the sake of their own generations. His point was that what edifying philosophers do is to challenge and problematize established ideas and ways of thinking, mainly by introducing novel redescriptions of the familiar: redescriptions that enable fresh approaches and alternative perspectives. Edifying philosophers offer the members of their respective generations new ways of thinking about themselves and their world rather than purported explanations of them and their world; edifying philosophers innovate truths rather than attempt to demonstrate timeless Truth.

How edifying philosophy applies to elective-death survivors' situations has to do with self-understanding: it has to do with productive appreciation by survivors' of how their EONs and iconic and coincidental cultures condition their cognitive and affective reactions to their loved ones who choose to die, and how those reactions may be changed by altering their fundamental perspectives. Old arguments such as Epicurus' about the utter irrelevance of the state of being dead, and even new arguments such as Todd May's contending that death as annihilation actually is preferable to death as transition to an afterlife, could be of use to survivors who are, for example, rethinking their positions on an afterlife.[10] But those arguments are not likely to prove of much help with respect to emotional acceptance of electors' choices. Against this, edifying redefinition and redescriptions that enable shifts in perspectives may be of inestimable help.

The crucial point to note is that what survivors need to accept or possibly to reject is not simply the finality of electors' deaths. By

---

[9] Rorty, Richard, 1980, *Philosophy and the Mirror of Nature*, Princeton, NJ: Princeton University Press, corr. edn., 369.
[10] May 2009. See the Appendix.

hypothesis, electors' deaths are shortly anticipated, even if they are not yet imminent, and survivors have no choice but to deal with those deaths. The finality that survivors need to cognitively and emotionally accept or reject in cases of elective death is not simply the deaths of their loved ones but that their loved ones are dying sooner than necessary and are doing so by choice. Survivors understand that their terminally ill spouses, partners, relatives, or close friends are soon to die; denial of that impending reality would be pathological to some degree. But what survivors may not understand and have serious trouble accepting is that their spouses, partners, relatives, or close friends are deliberately cutting short the time they have left.

Survivors tend to cope with electors choosing to die by focusing or trying to focus on electors' suffering. That is, they attempt to accept electors' choices to die by thinking or trying to think that electors really have no other choice than to cut short the time left to them and survivors think or try to think that they themselves would do the same in similar circumstances. However, while this tactic usually works at a superficial level, it seldom goes to the core of survivors' cognitive and affective states. The main reason is that at some level survivors see electors' choices to die as rejection or abandonment of their relationships with them. This is especially true of long-term spouses and partners. Survivors need to come to terms with what we can describe as an assertion of autonomy by their spouses, partners, relatives, or close friends: an assertion of autonomy in the sense that they are choosing to act in a way that does not give priority to their relationships with survivors.

To better understand the particulars of survivors' situations, we can consider a hypothetical conversation between an elector and a survivor. Returning to Edith and George, imagine that he has made sufficient progress in understanding his resistance to Edith's decisions to cease her treatment and to increase pain-relieving medication to discuss those decisions with her in a relatively cool and productive manner. We will take it that with treatment Edith could be expected to survive for rather more than our minimum survival time. Let us say that with treatment, Edith's prognosis is that she would live another six or eight months, whereas without treatment she most likely would die in four to six weeks or even sooner if pain-relieving medication is increased significantly. George and Edith might then engage in the following conversation or one very like it – and note the parts I have italicized:

George: "I've thought about your decision to stop treatment. I still feel it's wrong to take your own life, however indirectly, but I understand you don't believe that. I've also spoken to people who know more than I do and they assure me it's unlikely new treatment might become available in time. What I don't understand is *how you can just give up*. If I were in your place I'd want to hang in as long as I could just not to leave you."

Edith: "I know, I know, but you have to appreciate that it's not just the pain. I'm bone-weary of feeling like this; I can't do anything; I can't even read for more than a few minutes. I'm constantly expecting things to worsen; I'm groggy from the medication most of the time. I know I'm not going to get better, even for a little while. *I don't want to leave you*, but I can't go on like this."

I have italicized two brief passages in the conversation to indicate where George and Edith are being less than candid in the sense of not being wholly frank or giving complete expressions to what each is thinking or feeling. Nor need the lack of candor be only with respect to what is said to the other; each may not be being candid with themselves. The italicized passages represent what, in one form or another, would be present in the vast majority of similar conversations between electors and survivors.

What would almost certainly not be articulated, except possibly in anger, are a fundamental component of George's resistance to Edith's decisions and an equally fundamental component of Edith's thinking about her situation and options. Instead of George saying to Edith that he cannot understand: "how you can just give up," if he fully understood his own feelings and were being completely candid he would say that he does not understand "how you can turn your back on me and what we have together." And instead of Edith saying just "I don't want to leave you," if she also fully understood her own feelings and were being equally candid she would say: "I don't want to leave you and what we have, but it's no longer enough to make me continue existing as I am."

In other words, what George would not admit to Edith, or maybe even to himself, is that he sees her decisions to cease treatment and to risk much higher pain-medication dosages as denying him the time they might still have together, and so as not only deliberately ending but also devaluing their relationship for the sake of closure. For her part, what Edith would not admit to George, or maybe even to herself, is that her relationship with him is now simply insufficient to make it worthwhile for her to go on living as she is living and especially as she can expect to soon be living.

The essence of George's resistance is that by choosing to die, Edith is denying them time together. He knows she is going to die; he is not self-deceived about that, and he may even be prepared to face her death. But despite his cognitive understanding of her inevitable and impending death, as well as of her reasons for hastening her death, he may not be emotionally willing or able to accept – and perhaps to forgive – the hastening. More than likely, and possibly unrealistically, George feels that if their situations were reversed he would bear what she is unwilling to bear just to remain with her a little longer. In thinking and feeling as he does, George typifies how many, if not most survivors respond to their friends and relatives and especially their partners or spouses choosing to die in terminal illness.

What, then, do the foregoing considerations suggest with respect to the application of philosophical thinking to elective-death survivors' predicaments? It would be wrongheaded to maintain on the basis of general principles that philosophical arguments, say for or against the possibility of an afterlife, should and would invariably prove useful if properly employed and appreciated. Such claims are usually based on common but basically ungrounded assumptions that philosophical arguments are always relevant and invariably lend depth and objectivity to individuals' considerations. This is simply not the case. For one thing, more often than not pro and con philosophical arguments are employed to justify positions held rather than to reexamine and reassess them. The truth is that philosophical arguments for or against something seldom have much immediate bearing or effect on pressing and highly emotional concerns such as impending elective death, except when they provide intellectually respectable bases for beliefs already held.

What should emerge from George and Edith's hypothetical conversation is the central importance of what is at the heart of philosophical thinking and goes back to Socrates' admonition that the unexamined life is not worth living. Self-examination and reflection are crucial to survivors' coping effectively with electors' choices to die, and it is just here that what Rorty describes as edifying philosophy plays a most important role, for it allows redescription or reconception of basic aspects of individuals' EONs and hence of survivors' cognitive and affective perspectives on electors' decisions.

Philosophy offers elective-death survivors the incentive and means for productive self-reflection and redefinition. But the self-reflection is not and should not be psychological efforts at unearthing "real feelings" about electors' choices. That sort of reflection is what most counselors encourage, but it is to a large extent spurious in mostly manufacturing or at least heavily conditioning what it allegedly discovers. The main difference between dubious psychological reflection and the sort of edifying philosophical reflection Rorty espouses is that the former consistently assumes that there are "real feelings" to be unearthed beneath rationalizations and inclinations. Against this, philosophical reflection of Rorty's edifying sort begins with an understanding that feelings largely are functions of our perspectives and attitudes and how we define ourselves as persons and subjects, and therefore are open to change as perspectives and attitudes shift for various reasons only some of which reasons are reflectively accessible. The only productive sense we can give to the notion of "real feelings" is when individuals deny or rationalize what they are already aware of, and it is just here that redefinition and redescription can resolve such internal inconsistencies by altering the attitudes or perspectives that make what is denied or rationalized shameful or unwelcome.

In essence, edifying philosophical reflection applied by survivors dealing with elective death begins with getting clear on who survivors are as persons, not who they supposedly "really" are, but how they have defined themselves and especially how they have defined themselves in the particular circumstances of facing and trying to cope with situations as daunting as someone close to them choosing to die. This involves them looking hard at what may be illusions they have about themselves and their roles. It involves taking stock, as George had to do, of how their iconic and coincidental cultures have molded their ways of thinking about and responses to electors' decisions. In fact, edifying reflection is itself the beginning of redefinition. For instance, even initial reflection may make survivors realize that they have cast themselves as victims in one or another way, and that realization is the start of redefining themselves as allies or cohorts of electors making difficult decisions rather than as victims or fellow casualties.

The success of edifying philosophical reflection and attendant redefinition is, of course, dependent on survivors better understanding not only the influences on them of their iconic and coincidental cultures, but also their EONs and how their EONs make them who they are in general and in the particular circumstances. Once that understanding is achieved, even if only in part, it becomes possible for survivors to alter their perspectives by redescribing their roles in dealing with their spouses', partners', relatives', or friends' choices to die.

To illustrate the point, we can focus on a central aspect of George and Edith's case and note that George's apparent incapacity to accept that the relationship he and Edith share is no longer enough to make her cling to life is a result of his not seeing that their relationship has changed in a fundamental and irredeemable way. George is well aware that his and Edith's relationship has changed in the sense of being hampered in many ways by her condition, but he sees it only as hampered, he does not see it as basically at an end. If anything, he sees the core of their relationship as intensified and in some ways strengthened by her situation and what he considers their joint efforts to cope with it. And because of how he sees their relationship, George sees Edith's decision to die sooner rather than later as a choice to abandon what they have before she has to do so. This perception casts him in his own eyes as being denied a little more time to be her spouse or partner, as being denied a little more time to maintain their relationship. George knows Edith's death is inevitable, but he sees her death as occurring perhaps considerably later than it might if she continues treatment and avoids risky doses of pain medication. He may well understand that she no longer values her blighted life for itself, but he fails to see how she can no longer value it as the means of preserving and sustaining their relationship for a while longer.

We are assuming in this chapter that George has worked through his iconic cultural perception of Edith's choice to die as unforgivably sinful and his coincidental cultural unrealistic optimism regarding new treatments for Edith's condition. There is, however, another and much more elusive obstacle to his fully appreciating how his EON is conditioning his perception of both her situation and her decisions. This more elusive obstacle is that George has, in effect, cast himself as the victim of Edith's elective-death decisions. To clarify what I mean I need to borrow and to build on a point May makes regarding death, and I say "borrow" because I am not certain that I am using his point quite as he intended it. Nonetheless, what May says enables me to say more clearly what it is George is doing and what many survivors most likely also do in similar circumstances; it also enables better articulation of what I want to say about survivors' acceptance of the finality of electors' choices to die.

In the process of discussing how most of us avoid thinking about death, May observes that death,

when it comes, is always a shock, a blow from the outside, rather than the central human possibility. We react to death – that is, the death of others – as though it were something that happened to them, rather than something about who they are. If we saw [death] as the latter, we would equally have to see ourselves as mortal.[11]

George sees Edith's death as something that is going to happen to her, and his reaction to her decisions about her treatment and pain medication is therefore best described as his thinking that what she is doing is allowing what is going to happen to her to occur sooner than it needs to do so. This is the main affective source of his resentment and resistance regarding her decisions. George perceives Edith's prognosis and her decisions in a linear way: he sees her death from terminal illness as an event that is going to befall her in the fairly near future and her decisions as simply advancing the time when that event will befall her. He may understand her misery and distress, but sees them as bearable for a while longer, given what is at stake, and George no doubt believes firmly that if their positions were reversed, he would bear the misery and distress to stay with Edith as long as possible.

---

[11] May 2009, 41.

The point I am making is that George does not see Edith's death as something about who she is, as integral to what she is: a mortal being. As May puts it, George sees Edith's impending death as something that is going to happen to her, as an event that will befall her. And because he does not see her death as something about who she is, George in effect cannot see her elective-death decisions as her coming to grips with the impending realization of her "central human possibility." He cannot see that Edith is opting to realize that central possibility more on her own terms than in terms of the affliction that will otherwise end her life in due process. Edith is, as Nietzsche would have put it, appropriating her own death.[12] Assuming that after reflection prompted by her condition and prognosis Edith understands that her death is not just a forthcoming event but is something about her very essence that is soon to be realized, she is able to appropriate it and precisely not allow her death to be something that just happens to her.

What George needs to do, and why edifying philosophical thought is needed beyond even the best and most productive psychological self-examination and counseling, is to first understand his own death as Edith seems to have come to understand hers: as something about himself and not something that is going to happen to him. Only when George achieves this understanding will he fully grasp what Edith is doing in choosing to die. And if and when George does understand his own and Edith's deaths as something about them, not as events befalling them, he effectively will have redefined himself as a supportive partner or collaborator in her elective death rather than as a victim of it.

It merits mention that in discussions of death like this one, it is almost inevitable that some will attempt to enlarge and supposedly deepen the consideration of death, and to facilitate its acceptance, by contending that death can and should be made meaningful.[13] Purportedly, this is an admonition or exhortation to those facing death, whether their own or that of someone close, to take up an attitude toward the dying that puts it in an uplifting perspective.

---

[12] Nietzsche, Friedrich. 1954. *Thus Spake Zarathustra* (Part One, 1883). In Walter Kaufmann, ed. *The Portable Nietzsche*, New York: Viking Press, 103–439, 184.

[13] Sommerville, Margaret, 2010, http://www.theglobeandmail.com/news/opinions/finding-meaning-in-dying/article1428766/

On the whole such contentions are what used to be known as "pious thoughts" or what A. J. Ayer once called "wooly uplift."[14] These are remarks that while they express admirable sentiments, actually are of little or no practical use and sometimes are harmful in that they call for what cannot be achieved.

It is open only to a very few to give their deaths meaning or to recognize such meaning, as in cases of martyrdom for worthy causes or for the good of others or where deaths can be bestowed with significance generated by lives of special achievement or dedication or sacrifice. I mention this point about making death "meaningful" to distinguish it from the point I am making. I am not talking here about taking up a certain attitude towards one's death or that of a loved one and seeing it in light of accomplishments, successes, or other positive aspects of lives lived. I am talking about what is open to us all, which is to understand our deaths as something about us and not see them as events that befall us. If we achieve that understanding, then we can make death meaningful by appropriating it. As this applies in the present context, the point is that survivors' understanding of electors' deaths as realizations of what is inherent to them enables their grasping the nature of their own deaths, and that in turn enables survivors to grasp that electors precisely are appropriating their own deaths by not allowing their illnesses to make their deaths events that befall them. In the end, literally, it is this grasping of electors' intentions that enables survivors to accept the finality of the elective deaths of their spouses, partners, relatives, and close friends.

The key to how this acceptance works is that acceptance of finality is not just acceptance of the impending elective deaths of survivors' spouses, partners, relatives, or friends; in other words, it is not acceptance focused only on others, regardless of how close they may be. Rather, it is acceptance of finality that is first of all acceptance of one's own intrinsic mortality and only secondly acceptance of others' mortality. In fully recognizing and admitting their own mortality, in coming to see that death is something about themselves and not an extrinsic happening, survivors come to appreciate electors' choices to die. The acceptance may be prompted by electors' decisions, but it is acceptance rooted in realization of one's own inherent mortality

---

[14] Ayer, Alfred Jules, 1947, *Language, Truth, and Logic*, London: Victor Gollancz.

together with the further and perhaps more difficult realization that one's mortality can be appropriated by being willfully realized, that it can be made real by choice and not only by happenstance. Survivors' acceptance of finality regarding electors, then, begins with and in fact requires, if does not quite entail, survivors' acceptance of their own finality.

CHAPTER SUMMARY

Until relatively recently, philosophy underwent a period in which its conduct in North America and Western Europe tended to neglect death and dying as major concerns. The fairly recent interest in and expansion of applied ethics was a key factor in ending that neglect. A second key factor was what I describe above as a social maturing regarding death prompted by pressures on health-care systems, medicine's new ability to keep people alive, and media coverage of cases where people have chosen to die rather than allow terminal illness to destroy them as persons prior to obliterating them as living beings.

Traditional philosophy, as it turns out, has little to offer those facing loved ones' or their own deaths. On the whole, traditional philosophical treatments of death have focused on broad questions about whether death is or is not intrinsically an evil, whether there is some form of afterlife, on the nature of consciousness or what death may or may not end, and on ethical questions about self- and other-inflicted death. However, as indicated above, these considerations do not offer much to individuals facing their own deaths or the deaths of those close to them beyond affording them fundamental positions on the metaphysical and ethical possibilities.

Against this, edifying philosophy offers and invites redefinition and redescription by problematizing and challenging normal ways of thinking about death and elective death, as well as what is taken as established and rarely questioned about terminal illness and choices to die. In this way edifying philosophy enables personal changes in the form of shifts of fundamental perspectives and attendant attitudes, thereby facilitating adoption of new and usually more relevant perspectives and attitudes. In the cases that concern us, where survivors are dealing with their spouses', partners', relatives', and close friends' choices to die, edifying philosophy enables survivors to redefine themselves as helpers and even collaborators in their spouses', partners', relatives', and friends' elective deaths. The most central way edifying philosophical thought achieves this is by preventing or removing survivors' acceptance-precluding perceptions of themselves as victims.

Given the increasing likelihood, if not quite certainty, that more and more people will be in the position of being elective-death survivors in the future, we can only hope that as in Wittgenstein's prophetic observation, we will soon wonder why all of this needed saying.

Appendix

Belief in an Afterlife

The following consideration of belief in an afterlife and immortality is presented as an Appendix to the main text because it requires even more abstract notions and discussion than some parts of the preceding chapters.[1] Readers may opt to skip what follows, but given the numerous references to belief in an afterlife made in previous chapters, I believe that there exists an intellectual obligation to have a harder look at the issue of the possibility of an afterlife.

I maintain that where potential electors believe in an afterlife, the possibility of an afterlife must be acknowledged as only a possibility in deliberating elective death, and that belief in an afterlife cannot function as a fact or premise in the deliberation. However, I now recognize that Battin was right to point out that deliberation of elective death by those who do not believe in an afterlife should also include the possibility of an afterlife. However, the question that needs answering is just what that acknowledging the possibility of an afterlife amounts to and just what is believed when it is believed there is an afterlife. As will become evident, these are most difficult questions and their treatment not only requires recourse to philosophical abstraction, but also is one bound to prove controversial, particularly with readers holding religious beliefs. What follows, then, is an attempt to sort out as best I can the content

---

[1] Note that it is not necessarily the case that if there is an afterlife, it is eternal.

157

of belief in an afterlife and of acknowledgment that there might be one.

There are two basic issues or problems with believing in an afterlife and especially with believing in an eternal afterlife or immortality. Put most simply, there is the issue of what it is that purportedly survives death, and there is the issue of how long whatever purportedly survives might survive.

With respect to the first issue, Aristotle, that model devotee of balance and compromise, offered the view that our constitution as rational beings includes an "active" intellect and a "passive" intellect, and that it is active intellects that survive physical death but that passive intellects do not. The trouble with Aristotle's view is that the memories that define us as individuals are all in our passive intellects. What survives death, then, is something like a vital life force, our *élan vital*, but one that is totally impersonal because it holds nothing of us or our individual histories. Contrary to Aristotle's and views like it, the contemporary and historically traditional conception of an afterlife is grounded on and understood in Cartesian terms. In other words, the conception casts each of us as a substantial but immaterial mind or spirit or soul that is only temporarily attached to a physical body and is a separate substance from the material or physical substance of the body and independent of it. This idea is in Plato in essence, and it is the heart of most religious beliefs and doctrines about our basic nature and the survival of death.[2] Most briefly put, on this view we are contingently embodied substantial minds, souls, or spirits.

To understand conception of ourselves as immaterial substances, it is necessary to grasp the concept of substance as it was initially presented by Aristotle and later developed by medieval scholastic thinkers, but, most important, how it was influentially employed by Descartes. The heart of the Aristotelian idea is that there are two kinds of existents: substances and their properties. Substances exist independently of all else, while properties are wholly dependent for their existence on the substances they characterize. The qualification is that all substances are ultimately dependent on God for their being; God is the one and only substance that exists wholly on its own.

[2] However, see John Shelby Spong, 2009, *Eternal Life: A New Vision*, New York: HarperCollins.

What Descartes did with the idea of substance has defined popular and much of academic thinking about the nature of mind and body. Descartes' primary contribution was not so much to introduce but to make explicit the notion that substances not only have properties but have defining properties: that is, substances are what they are in virtue of essential properties that make them the substances they are. The import of this is that, for Descartes, the defining property of the substance of mind or the mental is thought, whereas the defining property of the substance of matter or the physical is extension.[3] This immediately separates us, as minds, from the material in a thorough-going way. We are separated out of the physical world and rethought as "in" it only in that we are – for a time – ensconced in bodies. In fact, the separation is so complete that Descartes then faces a formidable task in explaining how the mind and body interact.[4]

Beyond defining properties, substances have or may have numerous accidental or nonessential properties that may vary at different times and in different ways, but it is their essential or defining properties that make substances what they are. To amplify, in Aristotle, a person is a substance: a material entity, a living creature, defined by the property of being rational. However, persons may be short or tall, blue-eyed or brown-eyed, and differ in other ways. Nonetheless, what makes them persons is that they are rational; that is the defining property of human beings as substance. Descartes accepts the basic Aristotelian conception of substances and their defining properties, but he alters a key aspect because instead of conceiving of human beings as rational animals, and therefore as inherently embodied, Descartes conceives of himself, and so of other persons, as purely unextended mental substances defined only by thought and therefore independent of extension or the physical. This is the root of Cartesian mind/body dualism. Descartes abandons Aristotle's view of us as material substances having minds; for Descartes we simply are minds that – for a time – inhabit physical bodies of which we, as minds, are independent.[5]

---

[3] Note that we cannot say "extension in space" or that matter is extended in space, because Descartes did not believe there was space as something independent of extended matter. He believed the physical universe to be a plenum. See my *Starting with Descartes*, 2009b, London: Continuum Books.

[4] See Prado 2009b, chapter 4, 66–82.

[5] For a more detailed account, see Prado 2009b, chapters 3 and 4, 51–82.

The importance of the Cartesian view is that whether in naive or sophisticated terms, many if not most of those who believe in an after-life also believe that their essence as persons is separate from their bodies and hence their continued existence as persons is not a func-tion of the continued existence of their bodies. Dualism is currently out of favor among professional philosophers, but then the majority of them do not believe in an afterlife.

The embodied-but-separate view of us as essentially independent minds or spiritual in nature was and is not universally accepted among the religious. In Christianity, and particularly in Catholicism, the basically Cartesian/Augustinian conception of us as temporarily embodied spirits is opposed by Thomas Aquinas' conception of us as inherently both spiritual and physical beings. This Thomistic con-ception, at odds with the more widespread Cartesian/Augustinian conception, led to various theological debates and disputes. One of the more suggestive debates centered on Aquinas' doctrinal com-mitment to the resurrection of individuals' physical bodies at The Last Judgment. One particular question Aquinas addressed was how the body of a person who had been a cannibal and whose parents had been cannibals could be resurrected when at death it consisted entirely of parts of other peoples' bodies. Not surprisingly, Aquinas responded that in these rare cases God would create bodies *ex nihilo* for the spirits in question.[6] The issue may seem quaint to most con-temporaries, but it does indicate the implausibility of survival of death understood as the survival of embodied individuals. It is not surprising, then, that most believers in an afterlife believe in their survival as disembodied souls or spirits. We need to look a little more closely at the issue of what it is that purportedly survives death.

THE "WHAT SURVIVES" ISSUE

The rather paradoxical feature of Aquinas' conception of us as essen-tially embodied beings is that while it is a conception that raises very difficult questions for believers, such as the one about resurrection, it is also one that we more easily grasp to the extent that it does not

---

[6] Aquinas, Saint Thomas, 1952, *Compendium of Theology*, trans. Cyril Vollert. St. Louis, London: B. Herder, chap. 161, 172.

require trying to understand ourselves as substantial spirits. But this is a relative matter, one relative to our time. Three hundred years ago people no doubt more readily understood themselves as essentially spiritual and only for the interim embodied. What has changed is all we have learned about the brain and central nervous system and the shifts in thinking this acquired knowledge prompted regarding how we think of what we are. We must feel sympathetic with Aquinas, then, in his trying to think through how we might survive death as the beings we are and not as Dantean shades who were briefly ensconced in flesh.

Aquinas would have appreciated John Searle's efforts to explain how we are not Cartesian amalgams of minds and bodies but are, in fact, thinking bodies.[7] He also would have appreciated the problems Searle faces in trying to assert the total unity of the mental and physical without adopting a reductivist materialism that fundamentally casts experienced mentality as a complex but causally ineffectual side effect of brain and central nervous system activity. But whatever similarities there may be between Thomistic attempts to rethink survival of death and Searlean attempts to preserve the rich reality of our mentality while eschewing some form of dualism, Aquinas faces the daunting problem of saying how an essential part of us survives while another essential part of us ceases utterly to function and eventually decomposes. Eventual resurrection aside, it was incumbent on him to explain what happened to people's souls or spirits during the time between their deaths and the resurrection of their bodies. This daunting problem highlights the difficulty of understanding how we are what we are, much more than how we might survive death as what we are. It was in connection with this difficulty generally that Searle articulated his main interest in this way: "the philosophical problems that most interest me have to do with how the various parts of the world relate to each other[.]" Most relevant to our concern with belief in an afterlife is Searle's contention that theorizing about the mind "is in large part an attempt to answer the question, How does a mental reality ... fit into a world consisting entirely of physical particles in fields of force?[8]

7 Searle, John, 1995, *The Construction of Social Reality*, New York: The Free Press; Searle 1987.
8 Searle 1995, xi.

The answer Searle offers centers on his understanding of intentionality as wholly irreducible to physical goings-on.[9] Intentionality is the defining "aboutness" or directedness-on-objects of consciousness. Intentionality is mind's essential property, but it is not the defining property of a separate substance; it is a property of some matter having a highly complex structure. This conception of intentionality as intrinsic in consciousness and as irreducible to anything else determines Searle's ontological stand against behaviorism, causal-reductivist analyses of the mental, and all forms of reductive materialism that cast the mental as a mere causally produced by-product of neurophysiological events but one that has no causal effects on the neurophysiological processes that produce it. The irreducible nature of intentionality also determines Searle's opposition to cognitive science's functionalism and cognitivism, which are positions that basically equate thought or the mental with programs running in the brain and ignore consciousness as being only a kind of derivative phenomenon that plays no explanatory role in the production of behavior and so is only of subjective interest.[10]

The tricky part for Searle is not allowing the irreducibility of intentionality to entail Cartesian mind/body dualism. That is, the problem for Searle is not to allow irreducible intentionality to be or to be conceived of as a property of a substantial mind. Searle cannot allow intentionality to become or to be seen as the defining property of a substantial, immaterial mind. Intentionality must remain a property of specially organized matter: of matter that thinks. Searle insists that "mental phenomena are biologically based: they are both caused by the operations of the brain and realized in the structure of the brain."[11] What makes brains unique as material objects, then, is that because of their complexity they support states that inherently "point to" or are about things, events, and even other internal states – as when we are aware of and reflect on our anger or disappointment.

My invocation of Searle's understanding of the nature of mind is due to his being the most credible contemporary philosopher who rejects dualism but is not an avowed or tacit reductionist in holding

---

[9] See the discussion of Peter Goldie's use of intentionality in Chapter 1.
[10] Searle 1987, viii–ix.
[11] Searle 1987, ix.

one or another version of materialism that identifies the mental with physical events and allocates what we experience in thought to a subjective and causally impotent series of incidentally produced phenomena. Put somewhat differently, Searle's is a scientifically informed, contemporary conception of mind or consciousness that, while making mind or consciousness a property of the brain, does not reduce that property to matter in motion in the sense of identifying it with some material events. Therefore, Searle offers a cogent position on the mind or the mental that is fully up-to-date but avoids both reductivism and dualism.[12]

Does Searle offer anything with respect to answering the question of what it could be in or about us that might survive physical death? Some might be tempted to think that the property of irreducible mentality somehow attains a level that enables it to persist divorced from the material substance of which it was a property. For instance, I recall it being said of Wernher von Braun that he believed that we survive death as patterns of thought-waves.[13] If von Braun did believe this, his was an example of an attempt to understand an afterlife in physicalist-scientific terms. But the idea that our mind, our consciousness, might survive as collections of thought-waves or patterns on their own, that is, not inhering in matter, is one that is most implausible. Two things come immediately to mind about the idea: one is that there would be nothing to prevent eventual, if not immediate, dissipation; the other is that we seem to be back to Aristotle with this idea in that it sounds more like the survival of an impersonal force rather than of an individual identity. In any case, development of this idea requires far more be said about just how thought-patterns might survive on their own.

A little reflection makes it clear that the notion of an afterlife, of our survival of death as the persons we are, is more credible on a dualistic conception of mind and body. Cartesian understanding of essential selves as substances different from matter, and hence as essential selves that are only temporarily embodied, lends itself more to thinking that essential selves survive physical death. In short, whether it is religious or areligious, belief in an afterlife is facilitated

[12] Prado 2006.
[13] Although the particular reference, which I heard on a radio program, is not present there, see *http://en.wikipedia.org/wiki/Wernher_Von_Braun*.

by philosophical mind/body dualism to a much greater extent than by monistic conceptions. The facilitation can be described as a conceptual one, in that we cannot make sense of thought or of the mental – of our essential selves – surviving other than as substances of some sort: that is, surviving as entities that are not properties of something else, in this case of matter.

On the whole, it seems the most productive answer to the question of what it is in or about us that might survive physical death is that it must be a substantial mind: a Cartesian self that exists independently of matter, a soul or spirit that is different in kind from the body it inhabits for a time. The alternative, thinking of mentality as a property, means we would have to think in terms of mind or thought as a property of the brain and then becoming, at death, a property of something else material. But while that might enable an afterlife, it would preclude immortality. Even if we imagined ourselves as sequentially mental properties of a long series of different material things – for instance, migrating from galactic gas-cloud to gas-cloud – it is extremely difficult to further imagine that the process could go on forever.

The prospect that substantial minds survive death conjures up two possibilities of how such survival may be effected – not in the sense of achieved, since *ex hypothesi* the mind is independently existent as a substance, but in the sense of how survival would be realized. The first is the most difficult for many contemporaries to take seriously and is the fundamentally Platonic/Cartesian view that reality encompasses different kinds of substances each of which exists independently, and hence survival of the mind after the death of the body is simply a function of the mind's intrinsic existence as an independent mental or spiritual substance and so minds or souls or spirits would continue to exist on their own. The second possibility is one that has the mind attaching itself to other bodies or perhaps other things. This second possibility is the core of beliefs in rebirth, reincarnation, and transmigration. The substantial mind might also attach itself to a place, which is the basic idea of beliefs about hauntings. But both possibilities require that the mind or spirit or soul is itself a substance, that its continued existence is not as a property of something else, so both possibilities entail mind/body dualism.

Some might argue that the second possibility, where minds or spirits attach themselves to other bodies, things, or places, does not require that mind or spirit be an ontological substance in its own right. The argument would have it that the mind is a property, and that what changes with death is what the mind becomes a property of that supports its continued existence. The problem with this argument is that it raises even more questions about how the mind or spirit, as only a property, survives the shift from being the property of one body to being the property of another body or of something else. There also are at least as many questions about just how the shift is accomplished and whether the mind undergoes significant changes during the shifts.

However the property arguments may go, what is undeniable is that conceiving of the mind or spirit or soul as substantial requires an ontology that comprises at least two fundamental kinds of reality: mind and matter – three kinds if God is involved. This ontology further requires a complex metaphysics to explain the existence and particularly the interactions of the various substances. As alluded to above, we need only look at Descartes' *Meditations* to appreciate the difficulties of accounting for mind-body interaction and to further appreciate the hazards of postulating substances other than the material one in which we are so thoroughly immersed.[14]

Whether minds or souls or spirits are believed to survive the death of the body as substances in their own right or as properties that somehow attach themselves to other substances, we are inexorably brought to the second major issue regarding belief in an afterlife, which is how long it might go on.

THE "HOW LONG" ISSUE

Most readers will take it that the basic question here has to do with the problems mentioned in the last section, namely, with how long a mind might be able to transfer itself from one supportive substance to another or how long one or other of those supportive substances

---

[14] See Prado 2009b; see also René Descartes, *Meditations on First Philosophy*. Laurence J. Lafleur, trans., Indianapolis: Macmillan/Library of Liberal Arts, 1951.

might itself last. Perhaps surprisingly, that is not what the "how long" issue is primarily about; instead, the question is one about personal identity. Putting the question simply, how long might a mind or soul survive after death and still remain the same mind or soul? And "the same" here does not refer to the mind *per se*, as a substance or property. It refers to the person who is that mind. The promise of an afterlife would be as empty as impersonal survival of vital force if the person who initially survives death soon dissipates and the surviving mental substance comes to support – to actually be – another person. This question is much debated by philosophers concerned with personal identity.[15]

Perhaps surprisingly, the identity question is not only or even primarily a metaphysical question. Consider whether we can truly conceive of an individual identity lasting for, say, a million years, much less for an eternity. The key point to keep in mind is that an afterlife, survival of death, is essentially meaningless to us if it is not personal survival: if it is not *we* who survive. This means that aside from the no-doubt complex metaphysics involved, there is need to make sense of contentions about an afterlife in terms of individuals surviving as the persons they are, and this is not an easy matter.

I personally have never grasped how individuals might live, might continue to exist, for thousands of years, much less longer, and retain their identities as the persons they were at ages twenty, fifty, or even a hundred. I recall a science fiction story I read when still in grade school about people with unlimited life spans but who periodically had to undergo therapeutic regressions to childhood and, in effect, be reared anew as persons whose identities differed significantly from their earlier ones.[16] Recalling the story reinforces my difficulty in grasping how human memory, even enhanced and periodically retrained, could hold a life of a thousand years or more together so that the person who at age one thousand referred to herself or himself as "I" was still referring to the person he or she was at ten or thirty-five or ninety or even two hundred.

---

[15] For a succinct discussion of this debate, see Christine Overall, 2003, *Aging, Death, and Human Longevity: A Philosophical Inquiry*, Berkeley and Los Angeles: University of California Press, chapter 5, 155–82.

[16] Simak, Clifford D., 1951, "Second Childhood," *Galaxy Science Fiction*, Feb. 1951, 1(5): 83–98.

Consider the matter in terms of iconic and coincidental cultures and EONs or experience-organizing narratives and the changes individuals would have to make and assimilate if they lived for thousands of years or more. It beggars the imagination to think that anyone could live that long and continue doing the same things, whether it be in their work or recreational time, so they would undergo repeated assimilations of coincidental cultures. Additionally, they would need to adjust to continuous developments in their iconic cultures, as history shows us that even the most conservative cultures undergo some change or development. All of this means that their EONs would be periodically but endlessly refashioned to a greater or lesser extent. To appreciate something of the magnitude of accommodating such changes, think about older individuals presently adjusting to the changes around them prompted by advances in technology and the evolvement of social practices. It is difficult enough, now, for people in their sixties and seventies to adjust to changes in their social and technological environments. Consider that process of adjustment to change being continuous for decade upon decade and steadily intensifying due to advancements in science and developments in social structures. Values and morality, too, would inevitably change over millennia, as history shows us they have changed in the past, and also call for continuous adjustment.

Aside from the question about the survival of identity, some philosophers have argued that immortality is decidedly not desirable because of the unbearable tedium it would eventually bring.[17] Religion has an answer to the concern about the tedium of eternal or semieternal life, though it is not presented as such. Religion's answer also indirectly addresses the concern about identity. The clearest case that I know of regarding this answer is Catholic doctrine that holds that heavenly existence is not of infinite duration but rather is timeless. Problems with tedium and identity, then, do not arise because the afterlife does not involve duration at all. Instead, heavenly existence begins with transformation of the individual who enters heaven, and that individual's consequent existence then is one of timeless contemplation of the Beatific Vision. In this participation in the glory of

---

[17] May 2009, especially chapter 2. See also Overall 2003, 155–82.

God, no time elapses; contemplation of the Beatific Vision is as timeless as is its object of contemplation.

One complication with a religious conception of transformation and a timeless afterlife is that it fairly clearly entails a dualistic view of mind and matter. For Thomists, who hold that at the Last Judgment all individuals' bodies are resurrected, transformation would require transformation of the whole embodied individual. This means that timeless heaven would be partly populated with a number of material bodies. Here again religion has an answer, because of course the resurrected bodies would be perfected. However, this is one of those further steps that greatly increase the implausibility of the initial idea.

Personal identity and eventual tedium pose serious questions to the notion of an afterlife with respect to what it is that may survive death and for how long. But these questions hardly exhaust the difficulties with the notion. There also is an ethical question that goes to the heart of what is, for many, the whole point of an afterlife. Most who believe in an afterlife believe that in the afterlife people are rewarded or punished for their earthly behavior. That is, after all, what religious doctrines about an afterlife are all about. In the case of enjoying the Beatific Vision, for instance, its contemplation is something available only to those who enter heaven because of faith, sacrifice, and other forms of merit. Those who earn eternal damnation suffer a very different fate. And it is just here that the ethical question arises. Briefly put, can earthly behavior really merit eternal reward? And can earthly transgressions really merit eternal damnation? Is it fair to condemn someone to an eternity of suffering for actions committed during a cosmically insignificant life span? In a similar way, it is possible to ask whether things done and attitudes held during a cosmically insignificant life span can possibly merit unending contemplation of the Beatific Vision or its doctrinal variants. Nor does the ethical question arise only about reward and punishment for actions done and beliefs held or rejected. It also arises about knowledge and understanding. That is, it is a good question whether human beings, with all their limitations, are capable of fully appreciating the consequences of some or all of their attitudes and actions when those consequences are the achievement of eternal reward or the deserving of eternal punishment.

However, religious and ethical considerations aside, the "what" and "how long" questions are the ones that should give readers the most pause in the present context. It appears that those who believe in an afterlife have a number of philosophically loaded issues to deal with. One is an ontological issue with considerable metaphysical implications, and comes down to deciding whether what survives death is a substantial mind or spirit or soul, or what survives death is a mind or spirit or soul which becomes a property of something else. The other issue is whether the believed-in afterlife is eternal or not. If the belief is in immortality, then it is most likely that those holding the belief will further believe that the mind or spirit or soul that survives death is itself a substance. If the belief is in an afterlife of significant or great duration but not an eternal one, then it is most likely that those holding the belief will further believe that the mind or spirit or soul that survives death does so as a property of another body or of something else.

THE CONTENT OF CONSIDERING THE
POSSIBILITY OF AN AFTERLIFE

The aim of this Appendix is to amplify on the references and allusions to belief in an afterlife that are made in the foregoing chapters. The contention was made that deliberation of elective death by electors requires a crucial amount of objectivity about belief in an afterlife. On the one hand, it requires consideration that belief in an afterlife is just that, a belief, and not something that can figure in the deliberation as a fact or a given. On the other hand, deliberation of elective death also requires allowing for the possibility that there may be an afterlife, and incidentally that willfully ending one's own life may have significant repercussions if there indeed is an afterlife. The same is true about the possibility that death is personal annihilation, but the role of that possibility in electors' deliberations and survivors' responses to electors' choices does not pose nearly as many or as serious problems as does belief in an afterlife.

In the present context our main concern is survivors' responses to electors' decisions, so it is worth reiterating that survivors' assessments of electors' deliberations and choices to die also require awareness of the role played in those deliberations by belief in an afterlife. The most worrying aspect of this requirement for survivors is dealing with cases where electors' decisions to cease treatment or to end their lives by other means are prompted or significantly colored by a belief that on dying they will be reunited with a spouse or partner or finally accomplish things they were unable to do in life or a similar belief. Electors need to understand that while they have to consider the possibility of an afterlife, as well as of possible annihilation, in deliberating elective death, both possibilities are just that: possible outcomes following physical death. Electors cannot allow either possibility to function as a factual element or premise in their deliberations and choices without jeopardizing the soundness of their elective-death reasoning or motivation, and survivors need to be aware of when this sort of endangerment of reasoning and motivational soundness occurs.

Given what has been said above about the complexities and problems attaching to belief in an afterlife, what can we conclude with respect to how survivors and electors should deal with the possibility of an afterlife in deliberating elective death? We cannot expect to resolve even a few of the questions and issues considered, and these questions are by no means exhaustive of those that arise, so we need to articulate one or two basic points regarding the actual content of belief in and acknowledgment of the possibility of an afterlife in deliberation of elective death.

To begin with, the issue of how long minds or souls or spirits might continue to exist if they do survive physical death is the most speculative of the two main issues we are considering. This is underscored by the fact that it is arguable that we cannot in fact really conceive of immortality, of either an eternal or timeless afterlife. The strongest contentions about the afterlife being eternal or timeless, as well as about minds or souls or spirits being immortal either once they come into being and are embodied or prior to as well as after physical embodiment, are religious doctrines. As such, they are matters of faith and are held irrespective of full understanding – in fact, they are sometimes held despite lack of understanding. Concerns that what is claimed about an afterlife or immortality is or may not be intelligible will invariably be answered in terms of having to have faith in what is beyond human understanding. Fortunately, whether electors believe in an afterlife that is endless or infinite in time or in one that is timeless is not of primary importance with respect to the soundness of elective-death deliberations. As we will see below, what we require be acknowledged as a possibility can be formulated without reference to the duration or timelessness of an afterlife.

What are of primary importance regarding acknowledgment of the possibility that we survive death in one or another way are three things: first, that if there is belief in an afterlife, the belief is acknowledge to be a belief and not tacitly or explicitly taken as factual in elective-death deliberations; second, that if there is belief in an afterlife, the belief figure in deliberation as only a possibility; and third, that if there is no belief in an afterlife, the possibility of an afterlife nonetheless be factored into the deliberation of elective death. It is not necessary, and certainly not practical, that consideration of the possibility of an afterlife include consideration of its length or timeless nature. Our discussion of the "how long" issue, earlier, had as its point only amplifying on the questions that are raised by claims about an afterlife. It was not my intent, nor is it necessary, to make expectations about the extent of a possible afterlife part of elective-death deliberations.

Unlike the issue about the length or timelessness of a possible afterlife, the issue of what it is that survives death or is believed to survive death is highly relevant to elective-death deliberations. However, its relevance has less to do with electors needing to determine what they believe it is that survives death than it is because they need to understand what it is that they are allowing as a possibility, whether or not they actually believe in an afterlife.

As acknowledged in Chapter 5, individuals deliberating elective death need to allow for both the possibility that there is an afterlife and the possibility that death is personal annihilation. But as the foregoing discussion in this Appendix makes clear, the question of what it is that might survive death is a difficult one, and it raises serious questions about the content of belief in an afterlife and even the content of allowing that there might be an afterlife. It is for this reason that I suspect individuals who do not believe in an afterlife, and who deliberate elective death, cannot fully comply in their deliberations with the requirement that they allow that there may be an afterlife. The likelihood is that the closest individuals lacking belief in an afterlife come to allowing the possibility is one or another variant on the Aristotelian idea that an anonymous active intellect or *élan vital* somehow survives their deaths but that they, as the persons they are, cease to exist at death. Allowing this sort of vital-force possibility really is only a token gesture in allowing the possibility that there might be an afterlife. We have, then, some electors who most likely do not actually understand what they believe in believing in an afterlife, and other electors who most likely do not actually understand what they are allowing in acknowledging that there might be an afterlife and whose acknowledgments then are in effect vacuous.

What we need to do is articulate the minimal content of a meaningful acknowledgment that there may be an afterlife in order to enable those deliberating elective death to meet the required acknowledgment that there may be an afterlife. Articulation of that content will also provide the minimal content for the acknowledgment that death may be annihilation in that the latter acknowledgment will simply be the negation of the possibility.[18]

The key point regarding the minimal content of acknowledgments about the possibility of an afterlife is that what individuals deliberating elective death need to allow for is both that they might survive their physical deaths as the persons they are or that on dying they might cease to be the persons they are. Unfortunately, reference to individuals continuing or ceasing to be the persons they are on dying introduces still another complication, which is that elective-death deliberators need to understand that there is some possibility that in a sense they might survive death even though annihilated as the persons they are. This is the possibility of survival of an *élan vital*, raised by Aristotle, regarding the survival of the impersonal active intellect or the claims made by some religious sects that while at death persons cease to be, their life force rejoins a World Spirit or something of the sort. However, this complication only serves to support the point that meaningful acknowledgment of the possibility of an afterlife is acknowledgment of the possibility of personal survival.

---

[18] Some readers may feel these considerations should have been part of the revision of the criterion for rational elective death as developed in Chapter 4. I do not think this is the case because the considerations undertaken here are more detailed and more abstract than those involved in the revision of the criterion and would only have complicated matters if raised earlier.

As indicated, the question of how long persons might survive if they do survive their deaths is for all practical purposes irrelevant to consideration of the minimal content of the acknowledgment of the possibility of an afterlife. It does not matter how long persons might survive as the persons they are if they do survive death, so long as their survival is not just a moment or two that consciousness might continue before dissipating after physical death. What matters is that individuals considering elective death consider that it is possible that when their bodies are well and truly dead – when there is zero brain activity and zero organ function – they might still be conscious of themselves and of some environment for something more than the few moments consciousness might linger in a just-dead body. Of course, it also matters that individuals deliberating elective death consider that it is at least equally possible that their deaths are the annihilation of themselves as the persons they are – again, beyond the moment or two consciousness might linger after the death of the body.

The basic point here, then, is that it is integral to individuals' possible survival of death as the persons they are that they continue to be the same self-reflective beings they were prior to death. This is why survival as a vital force or something of that ilk is not relevant to sound elective-death reasoning and acceptable elective-death motivation. For our purposes, the core of both meaningful acknowledgment of the possibility of an afterlife and of acknowledgment of the possibility of annihilation is personal continuance.

It is interesting that most people contemplating their deaths, whether by choice or otherwise, think in terms of personal survival. As alluded to a number of times earlier, many think in terms of rejoining a previously deceased spouse or partner. This appears naïve to some, but it is in fact a good indication that meaningful survival of death is normally taken to be personal survival of death. There is some irony in the fact that it is the more sophisticated who raise the greater number of problems when it comes to what it is they believe or are allowing for in considering that there may be an afterlife, insofar as they usually try to understand an afterlife as impersonal because it then seems more credible and likely.

Regardless, then, of the complex issues that arise about a possible afterlife, the requirement that electors allow for both the possibility of an afterlife and of annihilation can be met readily enough if those deliberating elective death think in terms of surviving or not surviving death as the persons they are when doing the deliberating. The required content of the acknowledgment that there may be an afterlife or that death may be annihilation, therefore, comes to potential electors acknowledging that on dying they may or may not survive as the self-reflective persons they are when engaged in their deliberation.

The point of this Appendix was to clarify the notion of an afterlife and what it is that needs to be acknowledged in deliberating elective death. As such, the Appendix relates more to potential electors' deliberations than it does to survivors' responses to electors' eventual decisions. Can we close with some remarks that relate the points made more closely to survivors' situations?

The central point regarding survivors is that their roles with respect to electors' reasoning, motivation, and decisions is actually simplified if electors do think in commonplace terms of possibly rejoining a deceased loved one on dying or simply ceasing to be. If electors think this way, it indicates that they are thinking in terms of the possibility of an afterlife or of annihilation as personal survival or cessation. What is more difficult for survivors is if electors think in more complicated terms about possibly surviving death as a vital force or something of the sort. If electors are thinking in this more elaborate way, survivors likely face the need to influence electors' deliberations in order to make them realize that what is really at issue is their personal survival. This will prove an added burden for survivors, but it is an important burden because if electors are unclear about the possibilities of an afterlife or annihilation, their reasoning may well not be sound or their motivation may not be acceptable or both. More important for survivors themselves is that if electors are unclear about the survival/annihilation possibilities, electors' deaths will leave survivors wondering if they really understood what they were doing. It seems that, again, we can only have recourse to dialogue. Survivors must talk with electors and get them to appreciate the basic points made earlier. This call to dialogue, though, is not only or perhaps even mainly for the benefit of electors; it is really for the benefit of survivors because it is survivors that have to live with the consequences of electors' choices to die.

APPENDIX SUMMARY

As argued in Chapters 4 and 5, the soundness of elective-death reasoning and the acceptability of elective-death motivation require that deliberators acknowledge both the possibility that there is an afterlife and the possibility that death is annihilation. In this Appendix, the aim was to clarify problems with the former acknowledgment because it is not clear just what the content is of either believing in an afterlife or allowing that there may be an afterlife. The two main problems are the issue of what it is that survives death and for how long whatever survives might survive.

The issue of what it is that purportedly survives death rarely arises in most religious contexts because the underlying assumption as well as the doctrinal commitment is to each of us essentially being a soul or spirit that is immortal either after coming to exist as embodied or prior to and after being embodied. Even where there is doctrinal commitment to eventual resurrection of the body, what immediately survives physical death is a soul or spirit.

The issue of how long the souls or spirits that survive death might continue to exist is, in effect, too speculative to deal with productively. Again, doctrinal commitments generally are to souls or spirits being immortal. Problems regarding identity arise the moment the survival of a mind, soul, or spirit is postulated to survive for an extensive period of time or eternally. These problems are usually – and mostly only tacitly – dealt with in religious contexts by positing transformation of the surviving soul or spirit or by contending that the afterlife is not one of temporal duration but rather one of timeless adoration of or unity with God.

Belief in an afterlife is almost invariably influenced strongly by culture and especially religious training and background. And again almost invariably, it is an integral part of individuals' EONs. For these reasons, it may be difficult to get electors to think in terms of personal survival and that is what they need to allow for as a possibility in considering elective death. On the other hand, individuals who abandoned or never had a belief in an afterlife, and especially those who are adamant about death being annihilation, pose a problem in that their allowing the possibility of personal survival of death might be little more than an empty gesture. These are, of course, primarily problems for electors, whose elective-death reasoning must be sound and whose elective-death motivation must be acceptable. But they also are problems for survivors because they, like professional counselors, need to weigh and assess electors' reasoning and motivation. And of course matters are complicated when we factor in survivors' own beliefs regarding an afterlife. All that can be done is that both electors and survivors must limit themselves to understanding the possibility of survival and the possibility of annihilation as being possibilities of *personal* survival or annihilation.

Bibliography

Aquinas, Saint Thomas, 1952, *Compendium of Theology*, trans. Cyril Vollert. St. Louis, MO, and London: B. Herder.

Aristotle, 1985, *Nicomachean Ethics*, Terence Irwin, trans. Indianapolis: Hackett Publications, 1103b.

Audi, Robert, ed., 1995, *The Cambridge Dictionary of Philosophy*. Cambridge: Cambridge University Press.

Ayer, Alfred Jules, 1947, *Language, Truth, and Logic*. London: Victor Gollancz.

Battin, Margaret P., 2009, Review of *Choosing to Die: Elective Death and Multiculturalism*, *Notre Dame Philosophical Reviews*, Sept. 2009, http://ndpr.nd.edu/reviews.cfm (search archives for "Prado").

Boston, Wesley, 2003, *Feeling as the Self-Awareness of Emotion*. Queen's University, Kingston, Ontario. (This is Dr. Boston's MA thesis, which I had the privilege of supervising.)

Brooks, David, 2008, "The Behavioral Revolution." *New York Times*, Oct. 28, A23.

Camus, Albert, 1955, *The Myth of Sisyphus*. New York: Vintage Books.

Caplan, Arthur. 1981. "The 'Unnaturalness' of Aging – A Sickness Unto Death?" Arthur Caplan, H. Tristram Engelhardt, Jr., and James J. McCartney, eds., 1981, *Concepts of Health and Disease*. Reading, MA: Addison-Wesley, 725–37.

    1996, Interview on "The Kevorkian Verdict"; includes interview with Timothy Quill, courtroom coverage, and film of Kevorkian and individuals he assisted in committing suicide. *Frontline*, Public Broadcasting System (WGBH, Boston), May 14.

Choron, Jacques, 1973, Philip Wiener, ed., *Dictionary of the History of Ideas*, Vol. I. New York: Charles Scribner's Sons, 634–46.

Damasio, Antonio, 1999, *The Feeling of What Happens: Body and Emotions in the Making of Consciousness*. New York: Harcourt Brace.

de Sousa, Ronald, 1987. *The Rationality of Emotion.* Cambridge, MA: The MIT Press.

Dewey, John, 1930, *Human Nature and Conduct: An Introduction to Social Psychology* (edition with new introduction by Dewey), New York: The Modern Library.

    1988, "Experience and Education." In Jo Ann Boydston, ed., 1988, *John Dewey: The Later Works, 1925–1953,* Vol. 13, Carbondale and Edwardsville: Southern Illinois University Press, 1–62.

Descartes, René, *Meditations on First Philosophy.* Laurence J. Lafleur, trans., Indianapolis: Macmillan/Library of Liberal Arts, 1951.

Doidge, Norman, 2007, *The Brain That Changes Itself,* New York: Penguin Books.

Eire, Carlos, 2009, *A Very Brief History of Eternity.* Princeton, NJ: Princeton University Press.

Feldman, Fred . 1992, *Confrontations with the Reaper: A Philosophical Study of the Nature and Value of Death.* New York: Oxford University Press.

Foucault, Michel, 1971, "Nietzsche, Genealogy, History." In Paul Rabinow, ed., 1984, *The Foucault Reader.* New York: Pantheon Books, 76–100.

    1979, *Discipline and Punish,* Alan Sheridan, trans. New York: Pantheon.

    1980, *The History of Sexuality,* Volume 1, trans. Robert Hurley. New York: Vintage.

    1988, "Critical Theory/Intellectual History." Kritzman, Lawrence D., ed., 1988. *Michel Foucault: Politics, Philosophy, Culture: Interviews and Other Writings 1977–1984.* Oxford: Blackwell's, 17–46.

Frege, Gottlob, 1892. "On Sense and Reference." *Translations from the Philosophical Writings of Gottlob Frege.* Peter Geach and Max Black, translators, eds., 1952. Oxford: Blackwell Press.

Goldie, Peter, 2000, *The Emotions: A Philosophical Exploration.* Oxford: Oxford University Press.

Goldie, Peter, and Finn Spicer, 2002. "Introduction." *Understanding Emotions: Mind and Morals,* Peter Goldie, ed. 2002. Aldershot, UK: Ashgate Publishing Limited.

Griffiths, Paul, E. 1997. *What Emotions Really Are: The Problem of Psychological Categories.* Chicago: University of Chicago Press.

Hamel, Ronald, and Edwin DuBose, eds. 1996, *Must We Suffer Our Way to Death? Cultural and Theological Perspectives on Death by Choice.* Dallas, TX: Southern Methodist University Press.

Hartocollis, Anemona, 2009, "At the End, Offering Not a Cure but Comfort," *New York Times,* Aug. 20, 2009, 1, 16–17.

Hume, David. 1978. *A Treatise of Human Nature.* Oxford: The Clarendon Press, 415, 414.

Intersectionality, 2009, http://en.wikipedia.org/wiki/Intersectionality.

Iverson, Susan, Irving Kupfermann, and Eric R. Kandel, 2000. "Emotional States and Feelings." In Eric R. Kandel, James H. Schwartz, Thomas M. Jessell, eds. 2000. *Principles of Neural Science.* New York: McGraw-Hill.

Krausz, Michael, ed., 1989, *Relativism: Interpretation and Confrontation*. Notre Dame: University of Notre Dame Press.

Kuhl, Patricia, Barbara T. Conboy, Sharon Coffey-Corina, Dennis Padden, Maritza Rivera-Gaxiola, and Tobey Nelson, 2008, "Phonetic Learning as a Pathway to Language: New Data and Native Language Magnet Theory Expanded (NLM-e)," *Philosophical Transactions of the Royal Society B*, 2008, 363, 979–1000.

Leighton, Stephen, 2003 "Introduction." *Philosophy and the Emotions: A Reader*, Stephen Leighton, ed. 2003. Peterborough, ON: Broadview Press.

Luper, Steven, 2009, *The Philosophy of Death*. Cambridge and New York: Cambridge University Press.

MacIntyre, Alisdair, 1977, "Epistemological Crises, Dramatic Narrative and the Philosophy of Science." *The Monist*, 60(4), 453–72.

May, Todd, 2009, *Death*. Stocksfield, UK: Acumen.

Mullens, Anne. 1996. *Timely Death: Considering Our Last Rights*. New York: Alfred A. Knopf.

Nagel, Thomas, 1991, *"Death," in his Mortal Questions*. Cambridge: Cambridge University Press, 1–10.

Nietzsche, Friedrich. 1954. *Thus Spake Zarathustra (Part One, 1883)*. In *Walter Kaufmann, ed, 1954, The Portable Nietzsche*. New York: Viking Press, 103–439.

Overall, Christine, 2003, *Aging, Death, and Human Longevity: A Philosophical Inquiry*. Berkeley and Los Angeles: University of California Press.

Parker-Pope, Tara, 2009. "Treating Dementia, but Overlooking Its Physical Toll," *New York Times*, Oct. 20, Section D, 5.

Peritz, Ingrid, 2009, "Majority of Quebec Specialists Favor Euthanasia," *Globe and Mail*, Oct. 14: http://www.theglobeandmail.com/news/national/majority-of-quebec-specialists-favour-euthanasia/article1322669/

Perreaux, Les, 2009, "Quebec Medical College Cautiously Endorses Limited Euthanasia," *Globe and Mail*, Nov. 4.

Prado, C. G., 1984, *Making Believe: Philosophical Reflections on Fiction*. Westport, CT, and London: Greenwood Press.

   1990, *The Last Choice: Preemptive Suicide in Advanced Age*. Westport, CT, and New York: Greenwood Group.

   1995, *Starting with Foucault: An Introduction to Genealogy*, Boulder, CO, and New York: Westview Press.

   1998, *The Last Choice: Preemptive Suicide in Advanced Age*, Second Edition. Westport, CT, and London: Greenwood and Praeger Presses.

   1999, *Assisted Suicide: Theory and Practice in Elective Death*, with S. J. Taylor, Amherst, N.Y.: Humanity Books.

   2000a, *Assisted Suicide: Canadian Perspectives*. ed., Ottawa: University of Ottawa Press.

   2000b, "Ambiguity and Synergism in 'Assisted Suicide'," in Prado 2000a, 203–211.

   2000c, *Starting with Foucault: An Introduction to Genealogy*, 2nd edition, Boulder, CO, and New York: Westview Press/Perseus Group.

2003, "Foucauldian Ethics and Elective Death," *Journal of Medical Humanities*, Special issue, Vol. 24, No. 3–4.

2005, "Suicide and Power," *Symposium*, Vol. 9, No. 1.

2006, *Searle and Foucault on Truth*. Cambridge and New York: Cambridge University Press.

2008, *Choosing to Die: Elective Death and Multiculturalism*. Cambridge and New York: Cambridge University Press.

ed., 2009a, *Foucault's Legacy*. London: Continuum Books.

2009b, *Starting with Descartes*, London: Continuum Books.

forthcoming, "Educating the Self: Dewey and Foucault," in Paul Fairfield, ed., *Dewey and Continental Philosophy*.

Putnam, Hilary, 1987. "Why Reason Can't Be Naturalized." Baynes, Kenneth, James Bohman, and Thomas McCarthy, eds., 1987, *After Philosophy*, Cambridge, MA: MIT Press, 222–44.

Quill, Timothy, 1996, *A Midwife Through the Dying Process: Stories of Healing and Hard Choices at the End of Life*. Baltimore and London: Johns Hopkins University Press.

Quill, Timothy and Margaret Battin, eds., 2004, *Physician-Assisted Dying: The Case for Palliative Care and Patient Choice*. Baltimore and London: Johns Hopkins University Press.

Randall, William L., and A. Elizabeth McKim, 2008, *Reading Our Lives*. Oxford and New York: Oxford University Press.

Rhem, James, 2006, *The National Teaching and Learning Forum*, 15 (May), 1–4.

Rorty, Richard, 1980, *Philosophy and the Mirror of Nature*. Princeton, NJ: Princeton University Press, corr. edn.

1982, *The Consequences of Pragmatism*. Minneapolis: University of Minnesota Press.

Sack, Kevin. 2008, "Doctors Miss Cultural Needs, Study Says," *New York Times*, Tuesday, June 10, 2008, 12.

Schafer, Arthur, 2009, "The Great Canadian Euthanasia Debate," *Globe and Mail*, Nov. 6.

Searle, John, 1987, *Intentionality: An Essay in the Philosophy of Mind*. Cambridge: Cambridge University Press.

1995, *The Construction of Social Reality*. New York: The Free Press.

Schumer, Fran, 2009, "After a Death, the Pain That Doesn't Go Away," *The New York Times*, Sept. 29, 2009, Sec. D1, D6.

Solomon, Robert, 1980. "Emotions and Choice." *Explaining Emotions*, Amelie Oksenberg Rorty, ed. 1980. Berkeley: University of California Press, pp. 251–82.

Sommerville, Margaret, 2010, *http://www.theglobeandmail.com/news/opinions/finding-meaning-in-dying/article1428766/*.

Soyinka, Wole , 2002, *Death and the King's Horseman*. New York: W. W. Norton.

Spong, John Shelby, 2009, *Eternal Life: A New Vision*. New York: HarperCollins.

Stanford Encyclopedia of Philosophy, 2009a, *http://plato.stanford.edu/search/searcher.py?query=reason*

2009b, *http://plato.stanford.edu/entries/death*

Taylor, Charles, 1973/1985. "Self-interpreting animals." 1985. *Human Agency and Language: Philosophical Papers, I,* Cambridge: Cambridge University Press, pp. 45–76.

Young, Ernle W. D., 2008, "Choosing to Die: Elective Death and Multiculturalism," *Journal of the American Medical Association,* 300(14), 1703–04.

Williams, Bernard, 1976, *"The Makropoulos Case: Reflections on the Tedium of Immortality," in his Problems of the Self.* Cambridge: Cambridge University Press, 82–100.

Wittgenstein, Ludwig, 1980, *Culture and Value,* ed. G. H. Von Wright, trans. Peter Winch. Chicago: University of Chicago Press.

Works Not Cited but Relevant to the Text

Alvarez, Alfred, 1971, *The Savage God: A Study of Suicide.* New York: Penguin.

Ariès, Philippe, 1974, *Western Attitudes toward Death: From the Middle Ages to the Present,* trans. Patricia Ranum. Baltimore: Johns Hopkins University Press.

1982, *The Hour of Our Death,* trans. Helen Weaver. New York: Vintage Books.

Battin, Margaret P., 1982. *Ethical Issues in Suicide.* Englewood Cliffs, NJ: Prentice Hall.

1984. "The Concept of Rational Suicide." In Edwin Shneidman, ed., 1984, *Death: Current Perspectives,* 3rd edition. Mountain View, CA: Mayfield Publishing Co., pp. 297–320.

1990. *Ethics in the Sanctuary: Examining the Practices of Organized Religion.* New Haven, CT: Yale University Press.

Beauchamp, Tom L. 1980. "Suicide," in Tom Regan, ed. 1980. *Matters of Life and Death.* Philadelphia: Temple University Press.

1996, *Intending Death: The Ethics of Assisted Suicide and Euthanasia.* Upper Saddle River, NJ: Prentice Hall.

Belshaw, Christopher, 2009, *Annihilation: The Sense and Significance of Death.* Dublin: Acumen Press.

Benatar, David, ed., 2004, *Life, Death, and Meaning: Key Philosophical Readings on the Big Questions.* Lanham, MD: Rowan and Littlefield.

Blythe, Ronald, 1979, *The View in Winter.* New York: Harcourt Brace Jovanovich.

Borges, Jorge Luis, 1964, "The Immortal," in his *Labyrinths: Selected Stories and Other Writings* (augmented edition). New York: New Directions, 105–18.

Bresnahan, James F., 1993, "Medical Futility or the Denial of Death?" *Cambridge Quarterly of Healthcare Ethics,* 2(2): 213–17.

Brock, Dan. 1989. "Death and Dying," in *Life and Death: Philosophical Essay in Biomedical Ethics.* Cambridge: Cambridge University Press, 144–83.

Brown, Judy, 1995, *The Choice: Seasons of Loss and Renewal After a Father's Decision to Die.* Berkeley, CA: Conari Press.

Callahan, Daniel, 1987, *Setting Limits: Medical Goals in an Aging Society.* New York: Simon and Schuster.

Clark, Stephen R. L., 1995, *How to Live Forever: Science Fiction and Philosophy.* London: Routledge.

Choron, Jacques, 1972, *Suicide.* New York: Scribner's.

1963, *Death and Western Thought.* London: Collier-Macmillan.

Cowley, Malcolm, 1980, *The View from 80.* New York: Penguin Books.

Davidson, Arnold, 1986, "Archaeology, Genealogy, Ethics," in David Couzens Hoy, ed., 1986, *Foucault: A Critical Reader.* New York: Basil Blackwell, 221–33.

Donnelly, John. 1978. *Language, Metaphysics, and Death.* New York: Fordham University Press.

Durkheim, Emile, 1897, *Suicide: A Study in Sociology,* trans. J. A. Spaulding and G. Simpson . New York: Free Press, 1951.

Edwards, Paul, ed., 1967, "Intentionality," Roderick Chisholm. *The Encyclopedia of Philosophy,* Vol. 4. New York: Macmillan Free Press: 201–04.

Enright, D. J., 1983, *The Oxford Book of Death.* Oxford: Oxford University Press.

Epicurus, 1966. *Principal Doctrines,* in J. Saunders (ed.), *Greek and Roman Philosophy after Aristotle.* New York: Free Press.

Feldman, Fred, 1991, "Some Puzzles About the Evil of Death," *The Philosophical Review,* 100: 205–27.

2000. "The Termination Thesis," *Midwest Studies in Philosophy,* 24: 98–115.

Fischer, J. M., ed., 1993. *The Metaphysics of Death,* Stanford, CA: Stanford University Press.

1994. "Why Immortality Is Not So Bad," *International Journal of Philosophical Studies,* 2: 257–70.

Flew, Antony, 1967, "Immortality," *The Encyclopedia of Philosophy,* Vol. 4, Paul Edwards, ed., New York: Macmillan, 139–50.

Foucault, Michel, 1983. "On the Genealogy of Ethics: An Overview of Work in Progress," in Hubert Dreyfus and Paul Rabinow, *Michel Foucault: Beyond Structuralism and Hermeneutics.* Chicago: University of Chicago Press.

1997, "The Ethics of the Concern for Self as a Practice of Freedom," in Paul Rabinow, ed., and Robert Hurley, trans., *Michel Foucault: Ethics,* Vol. I of *The Essential Works of Foucault, 1954–1984,* Paul Rabinow, ed., 281–301. New York: The New Press.

Green, M. and Winkler, D., 1980. "Brain Death and Personal Identity," *Philosophy and Public Affairs,* 9: 105–133.

Hardwig, John, 2000, *Is There a Duty to Die? And Other Essays in Bioethics.* New York: Routledge.

Hamel, Ronald, and Edwin DuBose, eds., 1996, *Must We Suffer Our Way to Death? Cultural and Theological Perspectives on Death by Choice.* Dallas, TX: Southern Methodist University Press.

Hoefler, James, 1997, *Managing Death: The First Guide for Patients, Family Members, and Care Providers on Forgoing Treatment at the End of Life.* Boulder, CO: Westview Press and New York: Harper Collins.

Humphry, Derek. 1992a. *Final Exit: The Practicalities of Self-Deliverance and Assisted Suicide for the Dying.* New York: Dell.

1992b. "The Last Choice," review of Prado 1990, *Hemlock Quarterly*, October 1992.

Jean-Nesmy, Claude, 1991, "The Perspective of Senescence and Death," *Life Span Extension: Consequences and Open Questions*, Frédéric C. Ludwig, ed. New York: Springer, 146–53.

Kamm, F.M., 1988. "Why Is Death Bad and Worse than Pre-Natal Non-Existence?" *Pacific Philosophical Quarterly*, 69: 161–64.

1998, *Morality, Mortality*, Vol. 1, Oxford: Oxford University Press.

Kastenbaum, Robert J., 1992, *The Psychology of Death*. New York: Springer.

1991, *Death, Society, and Human Experience*. New York: Merrill.

Kluge, Eike-Henner, ed., 1993, *Readings in Biomedical Ethics*. Scarborough, ON: Prentice Hall.

1975, *The Practice of Death*. New Haven, CT: Yale University Press.

Kübler-Ross, Elisabeth, 1969, *On Death and Dying.* New York: Macmillan.

Ladd, John, ed., 1979, *Ethical Issues Relating to Life and Death*. New York: Oxford University Press.

Luper, Steven, 1987. "Annihilation," *The Philosophical Quarterly*, 37(148): 233–52.

2004. "Posthumous Harm," *American Philosophical Quarterly*, 41: 63–72.

2009. *The Philosophy of Death*. Cambridge: Cambridge University Press.

Lynn, Joanne, ed., 1986, *By No Extraordinary Means: The Choice to Forgo Life-Sustaining Food and Water*. Bloomington: Indiana University Press.

Martin, Raymond, 1994, "Survival of Bodily Death: A Question of Values," *Language, Metaphysics, and Death*, 2nd edition, John Donnelly, ed. New York: Fordham University Press, 344–366.

Nagel, Thomas, 1986. *The View From Nowhere*, Oxford: Oxford University Press.

Parfit, Derek, 1984, *Reasons and Persons*. Oxford: Clarendon Press.

President's Commission, 1981, *Defining Death: Medical, Legal, and Ethical Issues in the Determination of Death*. Washington, DC.

Quill, Timothy, 1996, *A Midwife Through the Dying Process: Stories of Healing and Hard Choices at the End of Life*. Baltimore and London: Johns Hopkins University Press.

2001, *Caring for Patients at the End of Life: Facing an Uncertain Future Together.* New York: Oxford University Press.

Savulescu, Julian, 1994, "Rational Desires and the Limitation of Life-Sustaining Treatment." *Bioethics*, 8(3): 191–222.

Seneca, 1969, *Letters from a Stoic*, trans. Robin Campbell. Baltimore: Penguin Books, Letter #77.

Spark, Muriel, 1959, *Memento Mori*. Harmondsworth, UK: Penguin Books.

Steele, Hunter, 1976, "Could Body-Bound Immortality Be Liveable?" *Mind* 85: 424–427.

Warren, James, 2004, *Facing Death: Epicurus and His Critics*. Oxford: Oxford University Press.

Index